Allah's name I begin with,
the utmost Kind, the ever Merciful.

THE BEAUTIFUL LIFE OF MUHAMMAD ﷺ

Muhammad Imdad Hussain Pirzada

AL-KARAM PUBLICATIONS

Title: The Beautiful Life of Muhammad ﷺ
Author: Muhammad Imdad Hussain Pirzada

ISBN 978-0-9569388-8-6

First edition: 1999
Second edition: 2016

Published by Al-Karam Publications
Eaton Hall, Retford, Nottinghamshire, DN22 0PR, England, United Kingdom
www.alkarampublications.com
info@alkarampublications.com

Special note of gratitude for Dr Muhammad Nawaz Mirpuri
for his work in translating this book in its first edition

Second edition translated from the original,
designed and typeset by Bakhtyar H Pirzada al-Azhari

Printed by Mega Printing in Turkey

Abbreviations:

ﷺ *Salla'Llahu 'alayhi wa sallam* (Allah bless him and grant him peace)
[*as*] *alayhi'l-salam* (upon him be peace)
CE Common Era
AH After *Hijrah* (the emigration)

CONTENTS

PREFACE

The Qur'an is the book of guidance, and the holy Prophet Muhammad ﷺ, who came to perfect human character, is the practical image of the Qur'an. In obedience to the holy Prophet ﷺ lies the obedience of Almighty Allah; in his following lies the love of Almighty Allah; in his actions lies the pleasure of Almighty Allah; in his excellences lies the gift of Almighty Allah; in his love lies the essence of faith; in his physical appearance lies the ascension of beauty; and in the life of the holy Prophet ﷺ lies a perfect example to follow.

No father today can find an example to follow in Prophet 'Isa (Jesus [*as*]), for he did not get married and have children. No labourer today can find an example to follow in Prophet Sulayman (Solomon [*as*]), for he lived the life of a king. But, *subhan Allah,* our Prophet, well he is a unique and matchless Prophet in this creation of Almighty Allah. In which scenario can you not find an example in the life of Prophet Muhammad ﷺ! The exemplar is everywhere. From a labourer to a king;

from a child to a parent; from a soldier to a commander; from a worshipper to the deliverer of sermon; from worshipping Almighty Allah in seclusion in the cave of Hira to being pelted with stones in the streets of Ta'if; from going into exile from Makkah in the dark hours of the night to conquering Makkah in broad daylight; and from herding a few goats in the mountains of Makkah to guiding thousands of people in the Farewell Pilgrimage. In short, the best and excellent example of the holy Prophet Muhammad ﷺ shines as bright as the full moon in every aspect of life. There is guidance for every dimension of human endeavour including the social, political, economic, cultural, ethical and religious.

When putting pen to paper in writing a book or exploring the *sirah* (prophetic biography) of the holy Prophet Muhammad ﷺ in some way, to restrict this unparalleled example to some historical events and episodes, and to ignore those great incidents and dimensions that create sentiments of love and obedience to this greatest guide, the holy Prophet ﷺ, in the hearts of people; this type of activity is in fact void of the actual objective of the *sirah*, in my view.

According to the needs of the present age, a book of *sirah* that is reflective of these two qualities, i.e. providing the factual details of the events in an analytical and academic manner as well as creating sentiments of devotion and affection towards the holy Prophet ﷺ in the hearts of the readers, is indeed the seven-volume book *Sirat Zia al-Nabi*. For this reason, I have the honour of including it in the *dars nizami* (higher Islamic studies) curriculum at Jamia Al-Karam. However, this masterpiece is very detailed and extensive for the young students of the secondary school. Thus, with permission from my noble and kind teacher, the author of *Sirat Zia al-Nabi*, Justice Pir Muhammad Karam Shah al-Azhari, the *Zia al-Ummat* (luminary of the community), I am presenting here a summarised and abridged version of those volumes of *Sirat Zia al-Nabi* that discuss the biography of the holy Prophet ﷺ. The manner of writing this book is simple, straightforward and easy to understand. Review questions at the end of the chapters will help the young students to learn and remember the beauteous aspects of the holy Prophet's life.

It is my aim that the young Muslims growing up in this part of the world create love in their hearts and obedience in their actions towards the holy Prophet Muhammad ﷺ by reading of his life, and also that they develop a passion to learn more and further pursue studies in the field of *sirah*. In this way, I am hopeful of my salvation in the hereafter. *Amin*.

The meaning, content and details of numerous narrations, events and *ahadith* (prophetic traditions) have been expressed briefly in this book. Therefore, for details and references, the readers are requested to refer to *Sirat Zia al-Nabi*.

مَوْلَایَ صَلِّ وَسَلِّمْ دَائِمًا أَبَدًا . عَلٰی حَبِیبِكَ خَیْرِ الْخَلْقِ كُلِّهِمِ
یَا رَبِّ بِالْمُصْطَفٰی بَلِّغْ مَقَاصِدَنَا . وَاغْفِرْ لَنَا مَا مَضٰی یَا وَاسِعَ الْكَرَمِ

Muhammad Imdad Hussain Pirzada
Founder & Principal of Jamia Al-Karam
Saturday, Jumada'l-Ula 29th, 1417 AH (October 12th, 1996 CE)
Eaton Hall, Retford, England, United Kingdom

CHAPTER 1

WORLD BEFORE ISLAM

The holy Prophet Muhammad ﷺ was born in 570 CE in Arabia. At that time people in the world believed in many gods. Some people worshipped stones; others had made animals their gods. Idolatry of this kind had spread to most parts of the world like an infectious disease. Man did not believe in the one and only Creator of the universe and had openly become rebellious.

Let us look at a few examples of the extent to which man had fallen into moral decline and how the holy Prophet Muhammad ﷺ was able to raise the moral state of man to its highest level.

IRAN

In Iran, the moon, the sun and wind were worshipped. Iranians followed the Zoroastrian religion. The sick were hated. A sick person was labelled as possessed by an evil force and no one went near him. He was left on his own to starve and die. Once dead, he was not buried, but was left hanging in a disused well to rot and be eaten by birds of prey.

Iranians considered cow's urine sacred and used it to purify impure objects. In the Zoroastrian religion, animals such as a dog had more respect than a wife or children. Marriage to your own daughter and sister was lawful. A rich man could marry hundreds of women. He could then handover any of his wives to his best friend rather like an ordinary object. The wife had no rights. She was treated just as an object of amusement.

ROMAN EMPIRE

Before Islam, the Roman Empire as well as its Byzantine Empire covered a vast area stretching from Britain to Egypt. Christianity was the official religion of the Romans. Non-Christians were treated unfairly, women were ill-treated and prostitution was widespread.

EGYPT

At one time each clan had its own god. Later Ancient Egyptians started to worship their kings. Marriage to your own daughter and sister (incest) was a common practice. Egyptians believed in life after death, but had rather peculiar burial rituals and ceremonies.

They would dig deep and construct several rooms in a mountain. They would lay the dead body of the king in the middle room. In the surrounding rooms the dead king's throne, his chair, jewellery, ornaments, water and large amounts of food would be stored up. These objects have been discovered by archaeologists in the twentieth century from the pyramids in Egypt. But they did not just stop at wastage of worldly goods and food in this way.

The Egyptians further believed their dead king would need the services of servants. They would leave a group of servants in one of the rooms and would close the opening into the tomb with large stones and sand. One shudders at the thought of the plight of those human beings left deep in the mountain, in the dark, with no water and food and with decreasing levels of air to breathe. What can be more cruel and unjust than to die such a painful and slow death?

India

Hindus had more than one god. They worshipped powerful things of nature. To them large mountains, rivers, seas, trees and even some animals were gods. The cow was a sacred animal to Hindus. They drank its milk but did not eat its flesh.

A group of Hindus, called Shoodar, were considered lowest of all Hindus. They were forced to live far away from the other Hindus. Shoodars were not allowed to go to religious meetings or read the Hindu religious books called the Veda. If a Shoodar was found reading the Veda, his tongue was cut and he was made dumb as a punishment.

Natural death of the husband was blamed on the wife. The wife was expected to lie down next to her husband's dead body and was burned alive. This cruel practice was known as Satti. If the wife refused to be buried alive in this way, then she faced a life full of hatred from relatives and friends. She was not allowed to remarry even if she was young. In some parts of India, several brothers had a common wife who lived with each brother for some part of the year.

CHINA

Chinese, like Hindus, worshipped many different objects of nature including mountains, rivers and wind. They would sacrifice law-abiding citizens and prisoners in order to seek favours from their many gods. Chinese worshiped dead kings too.

ARABIA

The people of Arabia had many good qualities. They had a very good memory. They were generous and charitable. They were brave. They were intelligent. They were trustworthy. Arabs loved poetry and were masters of the Arabic Language. However, these desirable qualities lacked guidance and were misdirected. Almost every household would mould stones into a statue and would worship this handmade idol as god. On long trading journeys, the traders would gather together a number of stones, select the one most pleasing to the eye and would treat it as god. The Arabs used to circle naked around the Ka'bah. They sometimes worshiped the sun, the moon, stars and fire. A relatively small number of Arabs believed in the one and only Creator of the Universe, Almighty Allah.

In some parts of Arabia, wives were freely swapped between men, and a woman could marry several men at a time. Daughters were not liked by the Arab society. In certain tribes, daughters were buried alive by the fathers. A father would feed, clothe and look after a chosen daughter to the best of his means until she was about six or seven years of age. At this age the father would ask his wife to dress up the daughter so he could take her to visit her grandparents in a distant village. He would take his daughter to a well in some remote corner of the desert and would ask her to look down into the well. As the girl would innocently lean forward, the father pushed her down into the well and quickly filled it up with sand. The poor and helpless child would scream and plead for mercy, but the cruel and barbaric father would have no mercy or shame.

Such was the state of the social, moral and religious decline of different human societies in the world at that time, when the holy Prophet ﷺ was born in the heart of Arabia.

Questions:

1. What were the beliefs of the people in 570 CE?
2. What religion did the people of Iran follow?
3. How were the sick people and dead bodies treated in Iran?
4. What is monotheism (*tawhid*)?
5. What is polytheism (*shirk*)?
6. What did the Egyptians believe about their dead kings?
7. How did the Egyptians bury their dead kings?
8. Who were Shoodars, and how were they treated by the rest of the Hindus?

9. What was the tradition of Satti in Hinduism?
10. List three good qualities of Arabs.
11. What did Arabs worship?
12. Describe how Arabs buried their daughters alive.

CHAPTER 2

ABOUT THE HOLY PROPHET ﷺ

In the Qur'an, Almighty Allah says:

وَمَآ أَرۡسَلۡنَٰكَ إِلَّا رَحۡمَةٗ لِّلۡعَٰلَمِينَ ١٠٧

"We did not send you (O Muhammad) but as a mercy for all the worlds." [Qur'an 21:107]

لَّقَدۡ كَانَ لَكُمۡ فِي رَسُولِ ٱللَّهِ أُسۡوَةٌ حَسَنَةٞ

"Surely you have an excellent example for your guidance in (the life of) Allah's Messenger." [Qur'an 33:21]

وَإِنَّكَ لَعَلَىٰ خُلُقٍ عَظِيمٖ ٤

"And verily you have the greatest character traits." [Qur'an 68:4]

The holy Prophet Muhammad ﷺ states:

إِنَّمَا بُعِثْتُ لِأُتَمِّمَ مَكَارِمَ الْأَخْلَاقِ

"I have been sent to practically set the highest standard of moral character." [*Musnad Ahmad ibn Hanbal*]

With reference to Sa'id ibn al-Musayyib, Imam Abu 'Abdillah al-Qurtubi writes:

"The holy Prophet Muhammad's community (*ummah*) is brought in front of him every morning and evening. The holy Prophet ﷺ recognises the face and the deeds of each and every one of his followers. Based on this firm knowledge, the holy Prophet ﷺ will bear witness to them all."

In *Tafsir Fath al-'Aziz,* Shah 'Abd al-Aziz al-Dehlawi writes:

"Your holy Prophet ﷺ will bear witness to you because with the light of prophethood (*nubuwwah*), the holy Prophet ﷺ knows the station, position in faith, nature of belief and the barrier that is hindering the promotion of his follower. Thus, he recognises your sins, level of faith, good and bad deeds, and your virtues and sins."

The reviver of the second millennium (*mujaddid alf thani*),

Imam Rabbani Shaykh Ahmad al-Faruqi al-Sirhindi writes:

"The birth of the holy Prophet Muhammad ﷺ is not like that of other human beings. In fact, it is not at all comparable to the birth of any man. This is because in spite of a physical birth, he was made from the light of Almighty Allah. And this is why he did not have a shadow."

Imam Sharaf al-Din al-Busiri in his poetry writes:

إِنَّمَا مَثَّلُوا صِفَاتِكَ لِلنَّاسِ . كَمَا مَثَّلَ النُّجُومَ الْمَاءُ

"The attributes and qualities of the holy Prophet ﷺ that they have presented to the people in words; that is actually like the reflection of stars in the waters of the sea, i.e. it is the reflection of the stars but the reality of the stars is still far greater."

Imam Abu 'Abdillah al-Qurtubi further writes:

"The real nature of the beauty and elegance of the holy Prophet Muhammad ﷺ had not been exposed to us. If it had, no one would have been able to see him. The eyes would have become devoid of sight, the hearts petrified and the purpose of the prophethood of the holy Prophet ﷺ would not have been fulfilled."

Justice Pir Muhammad Karam Shah al-Azhari, the *Zia al-Ummat* (luminary of the community), writes:

"The Creator in His divine wisdom allowed only the extent of exposure of the beauty and elegance of His Beloved ﷺ which people could endure; come near him and quench their thirst from his fountain of beneficence. It is not possible for a person to comprehend all aspects of beauty and elegance of Allah's Beloved ﷺ."

Justice Pir Muhammad Karam Shah al-Azhari, the *Zia al-Ummat* (luminary of the community), further writes:

"The garden of the world laid desolate and the pathways in ruins. The mind was about to explode with the unpleasantness of infidelity and polytheism. The feeling of despair was universal. Suddenly, a heavily vapour laden cloud rose above the peak of the mountain of Faran. As spring emerged, the garden welcomed every drop and sprinkle of mercy. The cloud rained down so abundantly that the earth glittered with the illumination of the Creator. The naked twigs became covered with leaves and fruit. The sad buds began to open out smilingly. In the garden of the world signs of life began to appear. The idols of falsehood came to an end. The turtle-dove, once again, began its melody purifying the heart and sight. From the high heights of purity and oneness (*tawhid*), the Huma (a legendary mythical bird) of humanity was being invited to fly high once again.

"The people of the earth called this personification of blessings and goodness by the splendid name of *Muhammad* (the one who is praised a lot), and the residents of the heavens called him *Ahmad* (the one who praises his Lord the most). But the whole truth only came apparent when the Creator and Sustainer introduced him to the world with the words: *"We did not send you (O Muhammad) but as a mercy for all the worlds."*

"The holy Prophet Muhammad ﷺ transformed the character and characteristics of his followers. They were ignorant, rude, ill-mannered, uncivilised and polytheists before embracing Islam. Islam transformed them into well-mannered, tolerant and cultured people and the founding fathers of a pure and praiseworthy civilisation. They had forgotten God, but then they lit the candles of belief in one Almighty Allah, the Creator. Thousands of praise and salutations be upon the holy Prophet Muhammad ﷺ who re-established man's link with his Creator and introduced to man the dignity of humanity."

The Companion, Hassan ibn Thabit, in his poetry in praise of the holy Prophet Muhammad ﷺ says:

وَأَحْسَنَ مِنْكَ لَمْ تَرَ قَطُّ عَيْنِي . وَأَجْمَلَ مِنْكَ لَمْ تَلِدِ النِّسَاءُ

خُلِقْتَ مُبَرَّءًا مِنْ كُلِّ عَيْبٍ . كَأَنَّكَ قَدْ خُلِقْتَ كَمَا تَشَاءُ

"My eye has never seen anyone more beautiful than you (O Muhammad). Mothers have never given birth to anyone more handsome than you. You have been created free from every defect. It is as though you have been created the way you yourself desired."

The Imam of the *Ahl al-Sunnah*, A'la Hazrat al-Shah Ahmad Raza Khan, writes:

تیرے خلق کو حق نے عظیم کہا - تیری خلق کو حق نے جمیل کیا
کوئی تجھ سا ہوا ہے نہ ہو گا شہا - تیرے خالق حسن وادا کی قسم
وہ خدا نے ہے مرتبہ تجھ کو دیا - نہ کسی کو ملے نہ کسی کو ملا
کہ کلام مجید نے کھائی شہا - تیرے شہر و کلام وبقا کی قسم

"Almighty Allah declared your manners to be sublime (O Muhammad); He created you in beautiful form. There has not been anyone like you and never will be; I take oath by the Creator of your beauty and elegance! It is God who has granted you this station that no one else got and nobody can get; such that the majestic Qur'an has taken oath by your city, your words and your existence."

It is narrated that Islam's worst enemy, Abu Jahl, had said:

كَيْفَ يَكْذِبُ عَلَى اللهِ وَقَدْ كُنَّا نُسَمِّيهِ الْأَمِينَ لِأَنَّهُ مَا كَذَبَ قَطُّ لٰكِنْ إِذَا كَانَتْ فِي عَبْدِ مَنَافٍ السِّقَايَةُ وَالرِّفَادَةُ وَالْمَشْوَرَةُ ثُمَّ تَكُونُ فِيهِمُ النُّبُوَّةُ فَأَيُّ شَيْءٍ بَقِيَ لَنَا

"How can we accuse Muhammad of saying falsehood when in fact we used to call him 'the trustworthy one'. He never told a lie. But the situation is that 'Abd Manaf (the family of the holy Prophet ﷺ) are already responsible for looking after the pilgrimage and distributing water to the pilgrims as well as assuming important advisory roles.

Now if prophethood also goes to them, then what is there left for us?"

Author of the book *The 100: A Ranking of the Most Influential Persons in History*, Michael H. Hart, writes:

"My choice of Muhammad to lead the list of the world's most influential persons may surprise some readers, but he was the only man in history who was supremely successful on both the religious and secular levels. Today, thirteen centuries after his death, his influence is still powerful and pervasive.

"We see that the Arab conquests of the seventh century have continued to play an important role in human history, down to the present day. It is this unparalleled combination of secular and religious influence which I feel entitles Muhammad to be considered the most influential single figure in human history."

Sir George Bernard Shaw writes:

"I believe that if a man like him were to assume the dictatorship of the modern world, he would succeed in solving the problems in a way that would bring the much needed peace and happiness. Europe is beginning to be enamoured of the creed of Muhammad. In the next century it may go further in recognising the utility of that creed in solving its problems."

Alphonse de Lamartine writes:

"If greatness of purpose, smallness of means and astounding results are the three criteria of human genius, who could dare to compare any great man in modern history with Muhammad?"

Alphonse de Lamartine further writes:

"Philosopher, orator, apostle, legislator, warrior, conqueror of ideas, restorer of rational dogmas, the founder of twenty terrestrial empires and of one spiritual empire, that is Muhammad. As regards all standards by which human greatness may be measured, we may well ask, is there any man greater than he?"

Mahatma Gandhi states:

"I become more than ever convinced that it was not the sword that won a place for Islam in those days. It was the rigid simplicity, the utter self-effacement of the Prophet, the scrupulous regard for pledges, his intense devotions to his friends and followers and his intrepidity, his fearlessness, his absolute trust in God and in his own mission. These and not the sword carried everything before them and surmounted every obstacle."

In his lecture delivered in Oxford titled *Islam and the West*, Charles, HRH The Prince of Wales, states:

"Cordoba in the tenth century was by far the most civilised city of Europe. Many of the traits in which modern Europe prides itself came to it from Muslim Spain. Islam is part of our past and our present, in all fields of human endeavour. It has helped to create modern Europe. It is part of our own inheritance, not a thing apart. More than this, Islam can teach today a way of understanding and living in the world which Christianity itself is the poorer for having lost."

Questions:

1. What did Almighty Allah say about the character of the holy Prophet Muhammad ﷺ?
2. Why did Michael H. Hart choose the holy Prophet Muhammad ﷺ to lead the list of the world's most influential persons in history?
3. According to Sir George Bernard Shaw, why is the creed of Muhammad important for the modern world?
4. Why did Alphonse de Lamartine say that the holy Prophet ﷺ was the greatest leader in history?
5. What was the reason for the spread of Islam according to Mahatma Gandhi?
6. According to Prince Charles, what is the role of Islam in the development of modern Europe?

CHAPTER 3

LINEAGE AND PARENTS

The first house of worship on earth is the sacred Ka'bah in Makkah, Saudi Arabia. It was built by Prophet Ibrahim (Abraham [*as*]) and his son, Prophet Isma'il (Ishmael [*as*]). Prophet Ibrahim's younger son, Prophet Ishaq (Isaac [*as*]), settled down in Syria and Prophet Isma'il [*as*] settled down in Makkah.

Of the many tribes that descended from Prophet Isma'il [*as*], Almighty Allah granted excellence to the tribe of Quraysh, and the most fortunate father amongst the tribe of Quraysh is 'Abdullah who was given the honour of being the father of the holy Prophet Muhammad ﷺ.

'Abdullah was the most handsome individual amongst the tribe of Quraysh and was a very modest and humble young man. He married Aminah who was the daughter of one of the leaders of the Quraysh, Wahb ibn 'Abd Manaf. Sometime after the marriage, 'Abdullah went on a trading journey to Syria.

Whilst returning from this trip, he fell ill in a place called Yathrib (Madinah) and passed away. *Inna lillahi wa inna ilayhi raji'un.*

The parents of the holy Prophet ﷺ were believers in the oneness (*tawhid*) of Almighty Allah and were followers of the way and religion of Prophet Ibrahim [*as*]. All of the holy Prophet's ancestors from Prophet Adam [*as*] to his father 'Abdullah and to his mother Aminah, through whom the light of the holy Prophet ﷺ was being transferred, were believers in one God and were pure people. None of them was a polytheist (*mushrik*).

The holy Prophet ﷺ was still in the womb of his mother when his father 'Abdullah passed away and so he set foot on earth as an orphan. Upon this, the angels said to Almighty Allah: "Your Prophet has become an orphan!" Almighty Allah replied: "I Myself am his Protector, and I am his Sustainer and Lord. You recite salutations and prayers of peace upon him and seek blessings by his name."

Questions:

1. Where is the first house of worship situated?
2. Who first built the Ka'bah?
3. Which one of Prophet Ibrahim's sons settled in Makkah?
4. Which one of Prophet Ibrahim's sons was the ancestor of the holy Prophet Muhammad ﷺ?
5. What is the name of the holy Prophet's tribe?

6. What is the name of the holy Prophet's father?
7. When and where did the holy Prophet's father die?
8. Who is Aminah?
9. What religion did the holy Prophet's parents follow?

CHAPTER 4

BLESSED BIRTH

It was 12th Rabi' al-Awwal, which was equivalent to 20th August, in the year 570 CE; the day was of Monday and it was the blessed moment of true dawn, when an eminent, great and orphan child was born to Aminah in Makkah. His name is Muhammad ﷺ. When the holy Prophet Muhammad ﷺ was born, he was already circumcised and his umbilical cord was already cut.

Aminah said that at the time of the holy Prophet's birth, the whole house became illuminated with his light. That light continued to spread everywhere to the extent that she could see the palaces of Syria in that light.

'Abd al-Muttalib said that on that particular night he was in the Ka'bah and he saw that the idols fell on their faces and then he heard a voice from the wall of the Ka'bah saying: "The Chosen One has been born, who will rid the Ka'bah of idols and establish the worship of only one God."

CELEBRATING THE HOLY PROPHET'S BIRTH

The holy Prophet Muhammad ﷺ used to fast on Mondays. When asked the reason for this, the holy Prophet ﷺ replied: "On this day I was born and on this day revelation was revealed upon me." [*Sahih Muslim*]

In other words, the holy Prophet ﷺ celebrated and expressed joy at his birth by fasting and in this way demonstrated gratitude and thanks to his Creator, Almighty Allah. The blessed birth of the holy Prophet ﷺ is a mercy for the whole world and a special blessing from Almighty Allah. Almighty Allah says:

قُلْ بِفَضْلِ ٱللَّهِ وَبِرَحْمَتِهِۦ فَبِذَٰلِكَ فَلْيَفْرَحُوا۟ هُوَ خَيْرٌ مِّمَّا يَجْمَعُونَ ﴿٥٨﴾

"Say: It is the grace of Allah and His mercy, upon which they should rejoice. This is better than everything that the people gather."
[*Qur'an* 10:58]

The followers of the holy Prophet ﷺ, the Muslims, have always continued to be grateful to Almighty Allah for this greatest blessing. On the day of the holy Prophet's birth, some fast; some perform voluntary prayers in seclusion at home; some come out in the open and proclaim his greatness; some distribute charity among the poor and needy; some decorate their homes and streets; some join in the gatherings of *milad* (*mawlid*) and listen to the beloved stories about the beloved Prophet ﷺ; and some recite salutations and prayers upon the holy Prophet ﷺ. In short the people of love in their own way thank Almighty Allah for this blessing.

There is a narration in *Sahih al-Bukhari* which mentions that when Thuwaybah gave Abu Lahab the news of the holy Prophet's birth, upon hearing the good news of the birth of his nephew, he was so happy that he freed Thuwaybah from being a bondmaid. Although Abu Lahab died as an unbeliever (*kafir*) and a complete *surah* (chapter) of the holy Qur'an was revealed in his condemnation; however, due to expressing joy and happiness at the birth of the holy Prophet ﷺ, he is given a sip of water every Monday in his grave, and his punishment is reduced on that day.

When an unbeliever who will forever remain in Hell, about him it is reported that every Monday his punishment is reduced due to expressing happiness at the birth of the holy Prophet ﷺ, then what do you think about that person who continued to express happiness at the birth of the holy Prophet ﷺ throughout his whole life and when he died, he died as a believer reciting the *kalimah* (declaration of faith)?

BLESSED NAME

On the seventh day after the birth of the holy Prophet Muhammad ﷺ, 'Abd al-Muttalib offered the *'aqiqah* (sacrifice of an animal out of joy at the birth of a child) and invited his relatives to a feast. When they had finished from their meal, they asked: "O 'Abd al-Muttalib! What have you thought about naming this grandson of yours?" 'Abd al-Muttalib replied: "I have named him *Muhammad,* so that Almighty Allah in the heavens and His creation on earth praise and honour this blessed child."

Whilst explaining the meaning of the Arabic word *Muhammad,* experts of the Arabic Language write that the one who possesses all good qualities and who is continuously praised, he is called *Muhammad*.

Questions:

1. When and where was the holy Prophet ﷺ born?
2. What is the name of the holy Prophet's grandfather?
3. At the time of the holy Prophet's birth, what did Aminah see?
4. What did 'Abd al-Muttalib hear on the night of the holy Prophet's birth?
5. Why did the holy Prophet ﷺ fast on Mondays?
6. How should the *milad* of the holy Prophet Muhammad ﷺ be celebrated?
7. What is *'aqiqah*?
8. Who named the holy Prophet ﷺ?
9. What is the meaning of the word *Muhammad*?
10. Why is the punishment of Abu Lahab in his grave reduced every Monday?

CHAPTER 5

FOSTER CARE

It was a custom of the Quraysh to let their babies be suckled by foster mothers from the oasis villages far away from the cities. The rural desert surroundings were considered cleaner and healthier than the cities and more beneficial for the physical and lingual development of young children. So the women from the villages used to come to Makkah every year and take away babies from rich families to look after them, suckle them and nurture them, and when the fostering period would come to an end, the parents of the children would reward them and give them numerous gifts.

'Abd al-Muttalib kept a look out for a foster mother who could suckle and nurture his notable grandson. During this time, a few women from the tribe of Banu Sa'd came to Makkah looking for babies to foster. Amongst these women was a lady by the name of Halimah Sa'diyah who had come to Makkah for this same purpose along with her husband, Harith. Halimah Sa'diyah tells her own story as follows:

"It was a year of draught and scarcity. We had almost nothing left with which we could survive. I set off from my home on a weak donkey with a group of women. We also took with us a she-camel but there was not even a drop of milk in her udder. My child was hungry and would cry all night; we could not sleep even for a moment. I had no milk left to offer the child and there was no milk in the udder of our she-camel too. Also when we had set off on our journey, the whole caravan was facing a nuisance, for my donkey was too weak to keep up with the rest of the group. They could not abandon us and carry on, nor could they travel at a good speed with us. We reached Makkah with great difficulty, and there the women quickly started going house to house looking for babies to foster. The women from the Banu Sa'd tribe did go to see the beloved son of Aminah, but they refused to foster her baby because he was an orphan. They thought that since there is no father, they would not be rewarded for their service, and that a widowed mother and an elderly grandfather would not be in a position to offer them a good fee and reward. After a few days all the women managed to find foster babies except me. No family was willing to let me foster their baby because I was so poor. I talked to my husband and we decided that it would be better for us to at least take Aminah's orphan son, rather than to return home empty-handed."

Halimah Sa'diyah continues: "I went to see Aminah who took me to the room where her beloved baby was resting. Seeing this beautiful boy of virtue and goodness, I was over-joyed and admired him greatly. When he opened his eyes, there was a sparkle and I felt that light was emerging from those eyes reaching the heavens. Instinctively, I kissed him between his eyes. I held him up to my chest and took him to my husband."

Halimah Sa'diyah says that when she arrived in her tent carrying this blessed child, her husband went to see the she-camel. He was very surprised to see her udder full of milk. He milked the she-camel and they were all able to drink plenty of it. That night they slept well. When they got up the next morning, her husband said: "By God! O Halimah! We have been given the most blessed child." "I hope so too," Halimah Sa'diyah replied.

Halimah Sa'diyah continues: "Once all the women were ready, we started the journey back home. All of the women with their new foster children rode on their same camels. I had with me that same donkey which could not walk well since it was so weak and which caused such a problem for everybody during the journey to Makkah. I sat upon the donkey with my beautiful foster son. But this time the same weak donkey suddenly became full of life and energy. She strode ahead of the rest of the caravan. The women shouted: "O Halimah! What has happened to your donkey? Is it the same donkey which could hardly walk! Where has she got the strength from?" I replied: "By God! It is the same donkey, but look who is riding it this time!" "

"Soon we reached our homes. Our area was very dry and you could hardly see a green blade of grass. Interestingly, when my herd of goats would return home in the evening, their bellies would be full and udders rich with milk. We would milk them and would drink as much milk as we wished. The herds belonging to other people would come home hungry with empty udders. They would reprimand their shepherds and tell them that they ought to take their herds where my goats grazed. We were very happy as day by day our fortunes changed and we became prosperous. Soon the two years had passed by quickly, and I weaned Aminah's beloved son off milk. During this time, his development and progress was unique. In two years, he became very healthy and strong."

Halimah Sa'diyah says that when people witnessed the blessings of Aminah's beloved son, they became very affectionate towards him. Whenever someone would suffer some physical pain, he would come to the holy Prophet ﷺ and place his hand over the aching part of the body, with the permission of Almighty Allah the pain would disappear. If a goat or sheep of someone would fall ill, they would stroke the animal with the holy Prophet's hand and the animal would become healthy again. Halimah Sa'diyah continues: "These two years of comfort and joy came to an end so quickly. Although our hearts were not ready for separation, since the time of fostering had come to an end, we brought the holy Prophet ﷺ back to his mother."

It is not possible to completely mention the countless blessings that Halimah Sa'diyah and her family experienced due to fostering the holy Prophet ﷺ. When the holy Prophet ﷺ married Sayyidah Khadijah, she gave Halimah Sa'diyah forty goats and several camels as a gift. When the holy Prophet Muhammad ﷺ declared prophethood, Halimah Sa'diyah, her husband and the rest of her family accepted Islam. The holy Prophet ﷺ always showed a great deal of respect for his foster mother. Whenever Halimah Sa'diyah would visit, the holy Prophet ﷺ would spread out his cloak and invite his foster mother to sit on it as a gesture of respect and affection.

Questions:

1. Who was Halimah Sa'diyah?
2. Why did the people of Makkah refuse to give their babies to Halimah Sa'diyah for fostering?
3. Why did the other women refuse to foster the holy Prophet Muhammad ﷺ?
4. What changes did Halimah Sa'diyah experience in her she-camel and donkey after taking the holy Prophet ﷺ?
5. Why did people from the tribe of Banu Sa'd become affectionate towards the holy Prophet ﷺ?
6. How did the holy Prophet ﷺ show respect to his foster mother?
7. What blessings did Halimah Sa'diyah receive by fostering the holy Prophet ﷺ?
8. What gift did Sayyidah Khadijah give to the holy Prophet's foster mother on the occasion of her marriage to the holy Prophet ﷺ?

CHAPTER 6

MOTHER AND GRANDFATHER DIE

Soon after his marriage, 'Abdullah went on a trade trip to Syria. On his journey back, he passed by Yathrib (Madinah) where he spent a few days staying there with the maternal relatives of his father, 'Abd al-Muttalib (since the mother of 'Abd al-Muttalib was the daughter of the leader of the Banu Najjar tribe of Yathrib). It was during this time that 'Abdullah fell ill and passed away there in Yathrib. Who can imagine the pain this news caused for the whole tribe of Quraysh and in particular for Aminah? How the grief-stricken Aminah would have desired to at least go and see the grave of her deceased husband? But it was the trust that she was carrying in her womb and its protection that did not permit her to travel to visit her husband's grave.

Thereafter, the holy Prophet Muhammad ﷺ was born. When the holy Prophet ﷺ was six years old, Aminah expressed a wish to travel and see the grave of her husband in Yathrib. 'Abd al-Muttalib agreed to this suggestion.

Taking her beloved son along with her, Aminah set out on a journey to Yathrib. They were accompanied by their maid, Umm Ayman. After spending around one month in Yathrib, when Aminah set out on her return to Makkah, she fell ill on the way at a place called Abwa' and there she passed away. Umm Ayman arranged her funeral and burial at Abwa', and then returned to Makkah with the holy Prophet ﷺ.

After the death of his mother, the holy Prophet's grandfather, 'Abd al-Muttalib, assumed all responsibility for his upbringing and care. But when the holy Prophet ﷺ became eight years old, his dear grandfather also passed away.

CARE OF ABU TALIB

After the death of his grandfather, the holy Prophet's uncle, Abu Talib, became his guardian. Although Abu Talib's financial position was not so good, nevertheless, he looked after his nephew and served him well. He loved the holy Prophet Muhammad ﷺ even more than his own children. He would always keep a watchful eye over him and even at night ensure he was sleeping nearby. At the time of dinner, no one would start eating without the holy Prophet ﷺ. With the presence of the holy Prophet ﷺ, the meal would always be blessed. If on an odd occasion, Abu Talib's children ate their dinner without the holy Prophet ﷺ, they would remain hungry and unsatisfied. But in the presence of the holy Prophet ﷺ, they would all eat well and always leave the dinner satisfied with some surplus food left over. Seeing this, Abu Talib used to say: "O my son! You are the most blessed."

Questions:

1. Where did Aminah pass away?
2. Why did Aminah travel to Yathrib?
3. How old was the holy Prophet Muhammad when 'Abd al-Muttalib died?
4. Who looked after the holy Prophet after the death of his grandfather?
5. What did Abu Talib used to say about his nephew?

CHAPTER 7

JOURNEY TO SYRIA

When the holy Prophet Muhammad ﷺ was about ten years old, he began to look after other people's herds in return for a fee so that he could help his uncle Abu Talib financially. At the age of twelve, the holy Prophet ﷺ went on a trade journey to Syria accompanying Abu Talib. Their caravan reached the valley of Bosra. Here, a Christian monk named Bahira observed an interesting event. Looking out from his monastery he saw that a cloud always provided shade over a child in the trading caravan. This cloud would always stay above this boy; wherever the boy would go, the cloud would follow.

Upon seeing this spectacle from his monastery, Bahira thought that this child could be the honest and truthful Prophet they were waiting for and whose signs had been mentioned in their books, and so it was important to have a closer look and become certain of those signs. Consequently, he came out of the monastery and went to where the caravan had pitched their tents. He then invited all of the people in the caravan to dinner. When they had all finished their meal, he bid the guests farewell and then went over to the holy Prophet ﷺ and asked several questions about how the holy Prophet ﷺ went to sleep, how he awoke, etc. Whatever details about himself the holy Prophet ﷺ would tell him, they would confirm the characteristics that Bahira already knew regarding the final Messenger who was to come. In the end, the monk lifted up the holy Prophet's garment from his back and began to look with interest at the birthmark, which was the mark of prophethood, on the holy Prophet's back. Bahira found the birthmark to be exactly the same as it had been described in his religious books. Immediately he leaned forward and kissed the blessed mark of prophethood.

Bahira then turned to Abu Talib and asked about his relationship to the child. Abu Talib replied that the child was his son. "No! That cannot be," said the monk. "This boy's father cannot be alive now," he continued. At that point, Abu Talib said: "This is my nephew."

Bahira then said: "Take your nephew and return back to your homeland. Remain watchful over him, for if the Jews see him and become aware of what I have become aware, they might try to harm him [since they were waiting for the coming of the final Messenger who they expected to come from the family of Prophet Ishaq (Isaac [*as*]) and not the family of Prophet Isma'il (Ishmael [*as*])]. Your nephew will have a great status. He is leader of all the worlds. He is the Messenger of the Lord of all the worlds, and Almighty Allah will make him a mercy for all the worlds."

Consequently, Abu Talib continued to Syria along with the

caravan. There he quickly completed his business and fulfilled his trade duties. He then returned to Makkah with the holy Prophet ﷺ.

Questions:

1. Why did the holy Prophet Muhammad ﷺ used to look after other people's herds?
2. How old was the holy Prophet ﷺ when he went to Syria?
3. Who was Bahira and why did he invite the Arab traders to dinner?
4. What did Bahira say about the holy Prophet ﷺ?
5. What did Bahira suggest to Abu Talib?

CHAPTER 8

PACT OF HILF AL-FUDUL

When the holy Prophet Muhammad ﷺ reached the age of twenty years, the youth of Makkah came together in an agreement taking an oath that they would stand against the oppressors to stop their oppression and they would aid and help those who were oppressed. This pact has been given the name *hilf al-fudul* (the alliance of the three Fadls), for in ancient times the tribe of Banu Jurhum had established a similar kind of pact, and the three prominent individuals in this pact had the same name, Fadl.

A Bedouin once came to Makkah with his daughter. A rich tradesman of Makkah kidnapped the girl and the father became greatly distressed. When the holy Prophet ﷺ heard of this incident, he gathered together the youth of Quraysh and encouraged them to help the Bedouin. Consequently, the youth came together next to the Ka'bah and they all took the following oath: "We hereby pledge to help the oppressed until they are able to take back their rights from the oppressors."

When the youth of Quraysh made this pact, the holy Prophet ﷺ was present with them. They washed the Black Stone (*hajar aswad*) with Zamzam water and drank the water. After this oath taking ceremony, the holy Prophet ﷺ led the group and went to the house of that oppressive tradesman. The youth surrounded his house and demanded that the girl be returned unharmed with dignity and honour. The tradesman asked if he could be given a night to think and he would return the girl to her father in the morning. But this was not acceptable to the young men and they rejected his offer insisting that he must return the girl to her family immediately. In the end, he was compelled and reluctantly returned the girl.

Due to events like this, the *hilf al-fudul* pact became very popular. Weak and oppressed people found help and support. Whenever anyone would wrong and oppress another person, the young men of *hilf al-fudul* would come to help and aid the person. Even after announcing prophethood, the holy Prophet ﷺ would remember this pact with great joy and satisfaction. He would say that if he was invited to a similar alliance even now, he would happily accept and be part of it.

Questions:

1. What was the objective of the *hilf al-fudul* pact?
2. Why was this alliance named *hilf al-fudul*?

CHAPTER 9

BLESSED MARRIAGE TO KHADIJAH

Sayyidah Khadijah was a virtuous lady of Makkah and a successful businesswoman. When the trade caravan of Makkah was making preparations to travel to Syria, Sayyidah Khadijah sent for the holy Prophet Muhammad ﷺ and informed him that she wanted to send her trading goods this year under his supervision and wanted him to look after her business interests in Syria. With the consent of his uncle Abu Talib, the holy Prophet ﷺ got ready to travel. Sayyidah Khadijah sent her servant, Maysarah, to accompany and serve the holy Prophet ﷺ during this trip. The business trip was greatly successful and this time Sayyidah Khadijah made a lot more profit than what was expected. Maysarah informed Sayyidah Khadijah of what he had witnessed with his own eyes of the holy Prophet's honesty and trust, trading skill and expertise, and the integrity and greatness of his character. So Sayyidah Khadijah sent a marriage proposal to the holy Prophet ﷺ. The holy Prophet ﷺ mentioned this to Abu Talib and eventually Abu Talib formally asked for Sayyidah

Khadijah's hand in marriage to the holy Prophet ﷺ from her uncle, 'Amr ibn Sa'd, since Khadijah's father had passed away.

In this way, with the consent of the elders of both bride and groom, the engagement took place and a date was agreed for the wedding ceremony (*nikah*). On the day of the wedding, the leaders and the elders of Makkah gathered together and Abu Talib delivered the holy Prophet's wedding sermon. The holy Prophet ﷺ was twenty-five years old at that time, and Sayyidah Khadijah was forty years old and she was a widow.

Sayyidah Khadijah gave birth to two sons and four daughters. The two sons, Qasim and 'Abdullah, died in their childhood. The four daughters, Zaynab, Ruqayyah, Umm Kulthum and Fatimah al-Zahra', witnessed the holy Prophet's prophethood and accepted Islam.

Holy Prophet's Sublime Character

Zayd ibn Harithah was kidnapped and later ended up being sold in the slave trade of those times. Eventually he was bought by Sayyidah Khadijah and was gifted to the holy Prophet Muhammad ﷺ. The holy Prophet ﷺ immediately freed him and treated him with kindness, love and affection like other children.

Meanwhile, Zayd's father was greatly distressed due to the separation of his son and began travelling to distant lands searching for his son who had been abducted. When he arrived in Makkah, he recognised his son Zayd. He came to the holy Prophet ﷺ and said: "Zayd is my son. I am ready to pay a ransom, so please free him." The holy Prophet ﷺ replied:

"Call your son Zayd and give him the choice. If he wants to go with you, I will let him go without taking any ransom from you. But if he prefers to stay with me and not to go with you, then you should not force him too."

Harithah responded: "You have been most kind! I accept this suggestion." Zayd was then called and was asked whether he recognised this man. Zayd replied: "Yes, this is my father." Zayd was then told that it was now his choice. If he wanted to go back home with his father, he could do so and if he wanted to remain with the holy Prophet ﷺ, he could happily do so too. Zayd immediately responded: "I am not prepared to leave you and go with anyone. You are like my father."

The strength, affection and integrity of the holy Prophet's sublime character had impressed and captivated Zayd to such an extent that he gave up his native country, family and everything else and chose to stay in the service of the holy Prophet Muhammad ﷺ.

Questions:

1. Who was Sayyidah Khadijah?
2. Who was Maysarah?
3. What influenced Sayyidah Khadijah to propose for marriage to the holy Prophet Muhammad ﷺ?
4. How old were the holy Prophet ﷺ and Sayyidah Khadijah at the time of their marriage?
5. How many children did the holy Prophet ﷺ and

Sayyidah Khadijah have together?
6. Who was Zayd ibn Harithah?
7. Describe the conversation that took place between Zayd's father and the holy Prophet Muhammad ﷺ?
8. What did Zayd's father want his son to do?
9. What was Zayd's decision?

CHAPTER 10

REBUILDING OF THE KA'BAH

During the year in which the holy Prophet Muhammad ﷺ became thirty-five years old, the Quraysh decided to rebuild the Ka'bah. The holy Prophet ﷺ took full part in this activity and himself carried heavy stones on his shoulders. People from different tribes were enthusiastically busy in rebuilding the Ka'bah in an atmosphere of love and dedication. However, when the time came for placing the Black Stone (*hajar aswad*) in the wall of the Ka'bah, this happy and cheerful mood suddenly began to turn into conflict between the different clans as tribal prejudice began to surface. Placing the Black Stone in the wall of the Ka'bah was a great privilege and each tribe wanted to have this honour.

Which tribe should have this honour? For four to five days continuously, the situation remained very tense and the danger of a bloody conflict became increasingly real. At any moment something terrible could have happened. At long last the chiefs of all tribes gathered together in *Masjid Haram*

(Sacred Mosque) to come to a final solution regarding this matter. They all agreed among themselves that they will spend the whole night there and whoever would be the first to enter the courtyard of the Ka'bah through the gate in the morning, he would be given the task of deciding this matter.

The next morning, the holy Prophet Muhammad ﷺ was the first person to walk through the gate. Seeing that it was the holy Prophet ﷺ who has come, the people were glad and overjoyed. When the holy Prophet ﷺ came to them, they informed him of what they had decided and that now it was up to him to settle the matter.

The holy Prophet ﷺ accepted their request and asked that a sheet of cloth be brought to him. The holy Prophet ﷺ spread the sheet out on the ground and with his own blessed hands placed the Black Stone in the middle of it. Then he invited each of the leaders from all the tribes to hold on to the sheet, lift it up and this way carry the Black Stone to the wall of the Ka'bah. They all took hold of the sheet. When they approached the point where the Black Stone was to be located, the holy Prophet ﷺ raised it with his own hands and firmly placed it in its rightful place in the wall. In this way, everyone gained the honour of participating in this sacred event.

Suddenly, the heated atmosphere which could have led to bitter chaos and conflict changed into one of heartfelt joy and happiness for everyone. As a result of his sublime character and noble characteristics, the holy Prophet ﷺ was already respected by the people of Makkah who referred to him with the noble and praiseworthy titles such as *sadiq* (truthful) and *amin* (trustworthy). However, by preventing a fiery quarrel among the tribes with this wise and prudent decision, the holy Prophet won their hearts even more as well.

Questions:

1. What is *hajar aswad*?
2. How did a conflict start between the tribes of Makkah when rebuilding the Ka'bah?
3. How did the holy Prophet Muhammad become the decision maker for the people of Makkah?
4. What was the holy Prophet's decision, and its effects?
5. How old was the holy Prophet when the Ka'bah was being rebuilt?

CHAPTER 11

PHYSICAL FORM AND CHARACTER

Almighty Allah always created His Messengers and Prophets free from all flaws and defects. None of them was crippled, blind, deaf or appeared dreadful, rather each one of His Prophets and Messengers was the most pleasant and beautiful individual of his time in every respect.

A Companion of the holy Prophet Muhammad ﷺ describes his appearance and physical form in the following words: "Allah's Messenger ﷺ appeared absolutely magnificent and very dignified to the eyes of the people. He was of medium build; neither too tall nor too short. His face was as radiant as the full moon. His forehead was broad and nose slightly lifted. He had a thick beard, shining teeth and a broad chest. When he would turn towards anyone, he would always give the person his full attention. When he would meet anyone, he would be the first to greet the other person. When a person would shake hands with the holy Prophet ﷺ, the other person's hands were left with a pleasant and sweet fragrance."

In his book *Kitab al-Tarikh al-Kabir*, Imam al-Bukhari quotes a narration from the Companion Jabir, who states that the Companions of the holy Prophet ﷺ could tell from where their beloved guide and leader, the holy Prophet ﷺ, had passed by due to the gentle and subtle fragrance that he left behind.

With a glimpse of the physical beauty of the holy Prophet ﷺ outlined above, let us also mention here something about his beautiful personality and noble traits of character. When the unbelievers of Makkah objected to the Qur'an and its message, the holy Prophet Muhammad ﷺ presented his own life as a proof of the truthfulness of the Qur'an. He asked them to look closely at his past forty years that he had lived amongst them. Every page from the book of his life was clear and open before them. Could they find even a speck of flaw in his character? What a great challenge this was! The people of insight and knowledge have so well said that for the first forty years of his life, our beloved Prophet ﷺ practically became the Qur'an demonstrating it to the people and for the last twenty-three years of his life, he recited that Qur'an to the people. In other words, he was the walking talking Qur'an.

'Abdullah ibn 'Amr reports that he used to write down everything that Allah's Messenger ﷺ would say, for he wanted to memorise those blessed words by heart. But the people of Quraysh tried to stop him from doing so telling him not to write everything. They said that the holy Prophet ﷺ is a human being, so he sometimes talks in a happy manner and sometime whilst angry. Consequently, he listened to them and stopped writing the words down. This whole event was mentioned to the holy Prophet ﷺ. The mercy for all the worlds, the holy Prophet ﷺ, pointed to his blessed mouth with his blessed finger and said to 'Abdullah ibn 'Amr:

اُكْتُبْ فَوَالَّذِى نَفْسِى بِيَدِهِ مَايَخْرُجُ مِنْهُ إِلَّا حَقٌّ

"Do write! By the One in whose hands lies my life! Nothing but the truth comes out from these lips."

In his words and in his actions, and through his social and business dealings, the holy Prophet ﷺ displayed very high standards of truthfulness, honesty and trust, such that the whole community began to refer to him with the noble titles of *sadiq* (truthful) and *amin* (trustworthy). Even the disgraceful enemy Abu Jahl would say to his very close friends that no one can doubt Muhammad's honesty and truthfulness, but the issue is that if his prophethood is acknowledged, they will end up losing their positions of leadership.

Questions:

1. Give a brief outline of the holy Prophet Muhammad's physical description?
2. Why did 'Abdullah ibn 'Amr stop writing down the *hadith* (the holy Prophet's words) and what did the holy Prophet ﷺ say to him?
3. Who gave the holy Prophet ﷺ the titles of *sadiq* and *amin*, and why?

CHAPTER 12

ANNOUNCEMENT OF PROPHETHOOD

When the holy Prophet Muhammad ﷺ reached the age of forty years, signs of prophethood (*nubuwwah*) began to appear in the form of true dreams. Whatever dream he would see in his sleep during the night, the next day it would come true. When he would go out of Makkah into the desert and the valleys, stones and trees would greet him with salutations, saying: "Peace and blessings be upon you, O Allah's Messenger!" The holy Prophet ﷺ once said: "I know a stone in Makkah which used to greet me with salutations of peace even before revelation upon me had commenced." Upon experiencing these signs, the heart of the holy Prophet ﷺ then became inclined towards solitude and he wanted to be alone. He would often go to the cave of Hira and worship Almighty Allah in seclusion.

This continued until it was the month of Ramadan, whilst the holy Prophet Muhammad ﷺ was engaged in the worship of Almighty Allah in the cave of Hira, that the archangel Jibril

(Gabriel) appeared in front of him and said: "Read!" The holy Prophet ﷺ replied: "I am not to read." Jibril repeated his request three times and each time the holy Prophet ﷺ responded with the same answer. On the fourth time, Jibril said the name of Almighty Allah with the request to read and asked to recite the full five verses. Although the holy Prophet ﷺ was not taught to read by anyone, nevertheless, by the blessing of Almighty Allah as a miracle he began to read:

ٱقْرَأْ بِٱسْمِ رَبِّكَ ٱلَّذِى خَلَقَ ۝١ خَلَقَ ٱلْإِنسَٰنَ مِنْ عَلَقٍ ۝٢ ٱقْرَأْ وَرَبُّكَ ٱلْأَكْرَمُ ۝٣ ٱلَّذِى عَلَّمَ بِٱلْقَلَمِ ۝٤ عَلَّمَ ٱلْإِنسَٰنَ مَا لَمْ يَعْلَمْ ۝٥

"Read, in the name of your Lord, who created (all); created the human being from clotted blood. Read, for your Lord is most Generous; who taught by the pen; taught the human being what he did not know." [*Qur'an* 96:1-5]

Bestowed with this honour of prophethood and following this first revelation, when the holy Prophet ﷺ returned home, he was shivering and his heart was shaking. He asked his wife Sayyidah Khadijah, the mother of the believers, to place a cloak over him. After a while, the holy Prophet ﷺ informed Sayyidah Khadijah of the whole incident that occurred in the cave and said that he was fearful and nervous in case he could not accomplish the duty of prophethood and completely fulfil the responsibilities of this great task. Sayyidah Khadijah reassured the holy Prophet ﷺ saying: "By God! Almighty Allah will never forsake you. You are kind to relatives; you help the weak; you spend from your earning on the poor; you honour the guests; and you help those distressed in the way of truth. A person who possesses these great qualities, Almighty

Allah does not abandon that person, rather Himself protects his honour and dignity."

SOME IMPORTANT TERMS

For beginner students of the prophetic biography (*sirah*), simple explanations of some key terms are presented here:

1. *Wahy (revelation):*
   In sacred law (*shari'ah*), *wahy* refers to that necessary knowledge which Almighty Allah creates in the hearts of the Prophets, whether that revelation is revealed directly without any means or indirectly through an angel.

2. *Nabi (prophet):*
   A *nabi* is that representative of Almighty Allah who has been granted knowledge of the unseen (*ghayb*) from Almighty Allah, such as Paradise, Hell, angels, etc. The number of noble Prophets is one hundred and twenty-four thousand (124,000).

3. *Rasul (messenger):*
   A *rasul* is that righteous individual who has been selected by Almighty Allah to convey His message to the people. The number of noble Messengers is three hundred and thirteen (313).

4. *Nubuwwah (prophethood):*
   The human eye is capable of seeing up to only a certain distance and making observations up to a certain limit. To comprehend beyond these sensory perceptions, intellect and reason are needed. But the scope of intellect

and its understanding have a finite limit too. To access the knowledge of realities and mysteries that lie beyond this reach, prophethood is needed. Prophethood is such a shining eye that through its radiance those hidden matters and realities of the unseen become visible that are far beyond the normal scope of human intellect.

5. *Mu'jizah (miracle):*
   The individual who is selected by Almighty Allah for the position of prophethood happens to be the most respectable and honourable individual among his nation. But when he proclaims his prophethood that Almighty Allah has selected him for the guidance of people, then people begin to demand proof to determine the truthfulness of his claim. Hence Almighty Allah grants to His Prophet such power and strength by which he becomes able to fulfil the demands of his nation. This power granted only by Almighty Allah is referred to as *mu'jizah* and it can be briefly defined as an act that occurs contrary to the normal custom and habit of nature. It is called a miracle because it cannot be enacted by an ordinary individual.

Questions:

1. Where is the cave of Hira?
2. Why did the holy Prophet ﷺ go to the cave of Hira?
3. Who is Jibril?
4. What is the first revelation?

5. How old was the holy Prophet  when he received the first revelation?
6. What is the difference between a *nabi* and a *rasul*?
7. Define the word *mu'jizah*?

Chapter 13

Invitation to Islam

The Arabs had gone so far ahead in their unbelief (*kufr*) and polytheism (*shirk*) that they were unable to tolerate even listening to the talk of believing in one God, Almighty Allah, and to the idea of abandoning their idols which numbered in their hundreds. This is why during the first year following the announcement of prophethood, the mercy for the world, the holy Prophet Muhammad ﷺ, kept his preaching secret and invited only selected and specific people to Islam.

Soon upright and decent people began entering the folds of Islam. The centre of these early preaching activities was the house of the holy Prophet's selfless Companion, Arqam.

The first to accept Islam was Sayyidah Khadijah, the mother of the believers, and after her the first to accept Islam among men was Abu Bakr; among children it was 'Ali; among freed slaves it was Zayd ibn Harithah; and the first to accept Islam among slaves was Bilal.

During that time of ignorance, it was not an easy thing at all for someone to leave the religion of his forefathers and accept the religion of Islam. Whoever would accept Islam, his whole family and tribe would turn against him. Mountains of troubles and difficulties would fall upon him and no moment of oppression and cruelty would be spared. In spite of that, whoever once grasped the blessed hand of the holy Prophet Muhammad ﷺ ended up selflessly devoted to him. May Almighty Allah shower countless mercies and blessings upon those pure and sacred souls who sacrificed their lives and everything they had for the sake of Islam. *Amin*.

ABU BAKR AL-SIDDIQ ACCEPTS ISLAM

Even before the announcement of prophethood, the holy Prophet Muhammad ﷺ and Abu Bakr al-Siddiq were good and close friends. They went together on several trade journeys. Abu Bakr was an eyewitness to the excellent traits and noble characteristics of the holy Prophet ﷺ and admired him deeply from his heart. So, when the holy Prophet ﷺ invited him to Islam, Abu Bakr immediately accepted Islam and became a believer. The mercy for the world, the holy Prophet ﷺ, himself used to say: "Everyone I invited to Islam contemplated, except Abu Bakr. He accepted Islam without hesitation."

Abu Bakr's original name was 'Abd al-Ka'bah. The holy Prophet ﷺ changed his name to 'Abdullah. It was due to the efforts and preaching of Abu Bakr that great individuals entered the folds of Islam, such as 'Uthman al-Ghani, 'Abd al-Rahman ibn 'Awf, Sa'd ibn Abi Waqqas, 'Abdullah ibn Mas'ud, and others.

HAMZAH ACCEPTS ISLAM

It was the second year after the holy Prophet Muhammad's announcement of prophethood. Hamzah was on his way back home after a hunting trip that a bondmaid stepped forward in the street and informed him: "O Hamzah! Today Abu Jahl treated your nephew (Muhammad) in a cruel and despicable manner. First he swore at him and then he beat him so badly that he started to bleed." Upon hearing this, Hamzah being a close relation to the holy Prophet ﷺ was shaken and he became very angry. He went straight to Abu Jahl and hit him hard with his bow, wounding him on his head. Afterwards, Hamzah went to see the holy Prophet ﷺ and said: "Nephew! You will be happy to hear that I have taken revenge from Abu Jahl for what he did to you." The holy Prophet ﷺ replied: "Uncle! I do not become happy with things like this. But yes, if you were to accept Islam, I would be very happy indeed." Immediately Hamzah accepted Islam.

'UMAR AL-FARUQ ACCEPTS ISLAM

Three days after Hamzah had accepted Islam, the mercy for the world, the holy Prophet Muhammad ﷺ, raised his hands before his Lord and supplicated:

اَللّٰهُمَّ اَيِّدِ الْإِسْلَامَ بِعُمَرَ

"O Allah! Help Islam by making 'Umar a Muslim."

Here, 'Umar ibn al-Khattab al-Faruq comes out of his house with his sword fiercely in his hand. Seeing the manner in which 'Umar was, a Muslim passer-by in the street asked him which way he was heading. 'Umar arrogantly replied that he was on his way to behead Muhammad ﷺ who had destroyed the peace of his city, Makkah, and had lit the fire of hatred in people's homes. The Muslim responded by saying that before continuing on, he should first see the state of his own household, for his sister Fatimah and his brother-in-law Sa'id had already recited the declaration of faith of this Prophet and had accepted Islam.

'Umar became furious at this news and instead of continuing on, he went straight to his brother-in-law's house. When he reached the house, he put his ear near the outside wall and tried to listen. He heard someone reciting something inside the house, so 'Umar shouted: "Open the door!" When the household heard 'Umar's voice, they became nervous, stopped reciting the Qur'an and carefully hid what they were reading. His sister Fatimah went and opened the door. Entering the house, 'Umar said in a roaring voice that he had become aware that they had abandoned the religion of their forefathers, and he then started to severely beat them to the extent that his sister and his brother-in-law both began to bleed. When the violent attack of 'Umar crossed all limits and became unbearable, his sister Fatimah could no longer hold back and passionately spoke out: "O brother! Beat us as much as you can. Our bodies can be torn to pieces, but we cannot give up the faith of Islam."

Hearing this response from his own sister drenched in blood, 'Umar's heart melted. "Sister! Show me what you were reading," he said. "You are impure and an unbeliever. Go and wash yourself first. Only then can you touch the scripture," replied Fatimah unreservedly. When 'Umar washed himself and read a few verses of the Qur'an, his heart and inner world transformed and he started to cry. Anxiously, he asked his sister to take him to the mercy for the world, the holy Prophet Muhammad ﷺ, so that he can accept Islam and find peace and tranquillity in his heart.

At that moment, the holy Prophet Muhammad ﷺ was sitting in the house of Arqam in the company of a few of his selfless Companions. Realising that 'Umar had approached the door with an unsheathed sword in his hand, the Companions hesitated in opening the door, but Hamzah spoke out: "Open the door. If 'Umar comes in peace observing the etiquettes of the holy Prophet's company, we will welcome him, otherwise we will chop his head with his own sword!" The door was opened and 'Umar walked in. The holy Prophet ﷺ supplicated once again: "O Allah! Rid the enmity for Islam that is in the heart of 'Umar and replace it with faith (*iman*)." After making this prayer, the holy Prophet Muhammad ﷺ said: "O 'Umar! Accept Islam!" 'Umar immediately without hesitation accepted Islam and became a Muslim. When the holy Prophet ﷺ heard this response, he was so happy that he loudly proclaimed *Allahu Akbar* (Allah is the Greatest). After the holy Prophet ﷺ, then all the Muslims together also loudly proclaimed *Allahu Akbar* such that it felt as if the streets and the atmosphere of Makkah resonated with the echo of this blessed sound.

After accepting Islam, 'Umar ibn al-Khattab said: "O Allah's Messenger! It is not appropriate now that this religion should be concealed." Consequently, the holy Prophet Muhammad ﷺ accompanied by the Muslims came out of the house of Arqam.

'Umar holding his sword in his hand was walking in front of the group loudly saying:

لَا إِلَٰهَ إِلَّا اللهُ مُحَمَّدٌ رَسُولُ اللهِ

"There is no god but Allah, Muhammad is the Messenger of Allah."

They entered *Masjid Haram* (Sacred Mosque) and 'Umar spoke out to the unbelievers of Quraysh: "Beware! If any of you tries to do anything, I will fight you with this sword." Such was this spectacle that the holy Prophet ﷺ performed the *tawaf* (circumambulation) of the Ka'bah and 'Umar walked beside him with his sword, guarding the holy Prophet ﷺ.

Before 'Umar had accepted Islam, thirty-nine men had entered the folds of Islam, and with 'Umar becoming a Muslim, the number of forty had now been reached.

Did Islam Spread by the Sword?

Those who allege that Islam spread with the force of the sword need to look deeply again and study the way these blessed souls, the early Muslims, embraced Islam. There was neither any promise or desire of worldly riches nor was there any compulsion by force or fear of the sword.

There was only the truth and veracity of Islam's message and the inspiring and exemplary character of the caller to Islam, the holy Prophet Muhammad ﷺ, which led these pure souls to stand against the forces of unbelief (*kufr*) and polytheism (*shirk*), and face mountains of oppression and cruelty.

Open Invitation to Islam

After three years of preaching in secret, the holy Prophet Muhammad ﷺ began to invite everyone openly to Islam. He stood up on Mount Safa and addressed all those who were present saying: "If I were to inform you that from the other side of this mountain, an army was marching forward coming to attack you, would you believe me?" They all replied that certainly they would believe him because they had always found him to speak the truth and never tell a lie. The holy Prophet ﷺ then said: "O people! Save yourselves from the torment of Hell and declare that there is no god but Allah."

Upon hearing this, Abu Lahab spoke out: "Damn you! Is this why you have called us?" The holy Prophet ﷺ kept quiet and did not respond to this insult, but his Lord, Allah, revealed a whole chapter (*Surat al-Lahab*) of the Qur'an in condemnation of Abu Lahab's disrespect, beginning with the verse:

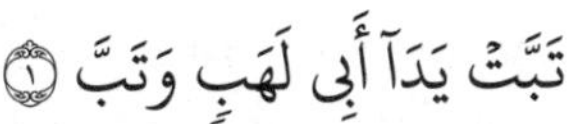

"Ruined be the two hands of Abu Lahab, and ruined is he!"
[*Qur'an* 111:1-5]

With this open preaching and invitation to all, the fire of rage and anger spread throughout Makkah. Those unbelievers who previously kept quiet due to some wisdom, now even they came out into the open in their opposition. They subjected the holy Prophet ﷺ and the Muslims to severe physical, verbal and emotional abuse. But despite this severe persecution Islam continued to spread.

Eventually the leaders of all the tribes gathered together, came to the holy Prophet ﷺ and said: "O Muhammad! You have created a serious problem for your people. Our unity has been shattered and you condemn our gods. If by this chaos you desire wealth, we are prepared to give you so much wealth and riches that you will become the richest man in the land. If you desire leadership, we will gladly make you our leader. And if you desire to have a crown and thrown, then tell us and we will all happily agree in making you our king. All we ask is that you give up your new religion."

The holy Prophet ﷺ replied: "If you brought and placed the sun in my right hand and the moon in my left hand, and expected me to give up the call to the oneness of God (*tawhid),* then this is impossible."

Disappointed from here, the unbelievers of Makkah then went to see Abu Talib. They said: "O Abu Talib! Your nephew condemns our gods, ridicules us and says that our forefathers are misguided. You either stop him from doing this or step away from the middle so that we can deal with him ourselves, otherwise we will declare war against both of you." When Abu Talib informed the holy Prophet ﷺ about his conversation with the unbelievers and this threat of theirs, tears filled the holy Prophet's eyes and he said: "The call to the oneness of God that I have embarked upon, I am prepared to die for it but I will not give it up." Abu Talib then replied: "Nephew! Do as you please, I will never abandon you."

When the people of Makkah had realised that their attempts to bribe and threaten bore no fruit, the situation became worse. The unbelievers got together and began to plan other ways of opposing and putting obstacles in the path of the holy Prophet ﷺ and the Muslims. During the month of the pilgrimage (*hajj*), they began to spread rumours and circulate misinformation among the people that would come to Makkah. They told people from other lands not to go near Muhammad ﷺ, for he was a magician who had the power to mislead people away from the religion of their forefathers. The unbelieving women of Makkah collected rubbish and would throw it on the holy Prophet ﷺ when he walked in the streets. When the holy Prophet ﷺ would prostrate in his prayer, the unbelievers would throw the stinking stomach contents of camels and dead animals on him and then would make fun of him.

The fortunate person who would accept Islam, his whole family turned against him. Some Muslims were forced to lie down on burning coal, others were thrown out in the scorching heat of the burning sun with their hands and feet tied together. For example, they starved Bilal of food and water, made him lie down on hot pebbles at the time of midday, placed heavy stones on his chest and told him to leave the religion of Muhammad ﷺ, otherwise he would continue to suffer like this until he died. Even when barely conscious, Bilal went on repeating: "Almighty Allah is one. I cannot associate any partner with Him."

Fate of Abu Lahab

After the Battle of Badr, Abu Lahab developed a dangerous boil on his skin which the Arabs considered to be a wicked and life-threatening infectious disease. When Abu Lahab's family found out that he had developed this foul condition, they all left him and separated. Left on his own, he continued to suffer the pain and distress for many days and then helplessly and agonisingly died. His body was left unattended for three days without a shroud or coffin.

When the body of this man who insulted the Messenger ﷺ began to decompose and the stench from his rotting body became intolerable for the local area, a man went to Abu Lahab's sons and cursed them saying: "Are you not ashamed? Foul smell is coming from the corpse of your father and you do not even bury him!" They replied that they were fearful of catching the disease from him. Eventually, out of fear that people will disgrace them, Abu Lahab's sons came, reluctantly pushed his body along with planks of wood and then pushed it down a hole, which they then filled by throwing stones into it from a distance. The word of Almighty Allah was clearly fulfilled. The whole world witnessed the disgraceful end of a man who was rude to Allah's Messenger Muhammad ﷺ, such that even his own sons were not prepared to go near him.

Questions:

1. Whose house was the centre of preaching Islam in the very beginning?
2. Who was the first to accept Islam among the women, the men, the children, the freed slaves and the slaves?
3. What was Abu Bakr's original name, and what was the reason he accepted Islam without hesitation?
4. How did Hamzah become a Muslim?

5. Describe the events that led to 'Umar al-Faruq becoming a Muslim.
6. Did Islam spread by the sword or by truthfulness and good character?
7. Who was Abu Lahab and what was his eventual fate?
8. What attempts did the leaders of Makkah make to stop the holy Prophet  from preaching Islam, and what was the holy Prophet's response?
9. In what way was Bilal made to suffer to keep him away from Islam, and what was his response?

CHAPTER 14

EMIGRATION TO ABYSSINIA

When the mercy for the world, the holy Prophet Muhammad ﷺ, saw that the violence and aggression perpetuated by the unbelievers of Makkah against the Muslims was not showing any sign of stopping and in fact the level of persecution was increasing, the holy Prophet ﷺ granted his selfless followers permission to emigrate to Abyssinia (Ethiopia) because the Christian King of Abyssinia, Negus (al-Najashi), was a fair-minded and considerate ruler. He does not oppress anyone and does not allow anyone to oppress the weaker ones.

So, in the fifth year after the announcement of prophethood, the first group of emigrants departed from their beloved homeland heading for Abyssinia. This group consisted of twelve men and four women. The group was led by 'Uthman al-Ghani, and his wife Ruqayyah, the daughter of the holy Prophet ﷺ, was also part of this emigration. When these travellers in the way of truth reached Abyssinia, Negus welcomed them well and provided them with a safe place to stay. Three months passed by in great peace and then suddenly a rumour circulated that the people of Makkah had all accepted Islam and it was safe to return home, and so the majority of Muslims in Abyssinia returned to Makkah. But when they returned they realised that these were just rumours, the situation of the Muslims was even worse than before in Makkah. Eventually the holy Prophet ﷺ granted permission to emigrate to Abyssinia again. This time the group consisted of Ja'far ibn Abi Talib and other Muslims too, and the number of people in this group was eighty-three.

When such a large number of Muslims had left Makkah for Abyssinia, the unbelievers of Makkah became concerned that the Muslims might gather their strength in Abyssinia and launch an attack on them from the outside. So, after mutual consultation they decided to send two ambassadors to Negus who would meet him and try their best in every possible way to influence him so that he expels the Muslims from Abyssinia and forces them to return to Makkah. These ambassadors took with them lots of valuable and elegant gifts in order to win over the king and his courtiers. Hence when they reached Abyssinia, the ambassadors of Quraysh pleaded with Negus saying: "Some fools from our city of Makkah have come to your country and settled here. They have abandoned the religion of their people and have not adopted your religion either. They have made up a new religion. We have been sent by the leaders of Quraysh to ask you to order them out of your country and to return to their homes and families."

Subsequently, Negus called for the noble Companions to be present in his court and asked them to tell him about the religion that they had adopted, for which they had abandoned the religion of their forefathers. In response, Ja'far ibn Abi Talib stated: "O King! We were an ignorant people. We worshipped idols. Almighty Allah has sent a Messenger to us whose lineage as well as his honesty and integrity we are well aware of. He has invited us to believe in the one God, Allah." Ja'far then recited a few verses from chapter 19 (*Surat Maryam*) of the Qur'an, listening to which moved Negus to tears and he became very emotional. Negus then said: "These words and the words revealed upon Prophet 'Isa (Jesus [*as*]) are two rays of light from the same sun."

Negus then turned to the ambassadors of Quraysh and told them firmly: "You go away from here. I am not prepared to hand these people over to you. The Prophet they believe in, I bear witness that he is the Messenger of Allah, and he is the same Messenger about whose arrival Prophet 'Isa [*as*] gave glad tidings. By God! If I did not have the burden of ruling my people, I would come to the holy Prophet ﷺ and would gain the blessings of pouring water for him during ablution."

Later on, when Negus died, the holy Prophet ﷺ performed his funeral prayer with his Companions in Madinah and supplicated to Almighty Allah for his forgiveness.

Questions:

1. What was the name of the King of Abyssinia?
2. Why did the Muslims emigrate to Abyssinia?

3. Who led the first group to Abyssinia, and what was the name of the holy Prophet's daughter who also went?
4. What did the unbelievers of Makkah decide when they found out that some Muslims had gone to Abyssinia?
5. What did Ja'far ibn Abi Talib say to Negus?
6. What was the King's reaction when he heard the verses of the Qur'an?
7. What did the King say to the ambassadors of Quraysh?

CHAPTER 15

SOCIAL BOYCOTT

The unbelievers of Makkah had the false perception that due to their aggression, terror and persecution, they will be able to put an end to the movement of Islam. Despite all of their cruel efforts and harsh tactics, the religion of Islam was continually succeeding. This was now intolerable for them. So, they met together and came to the conclusion that the only sure way to put an end to the spread of Islam and end their miseries was to end the life of the holy Prophet Muhammad ﷺ.

When Abu Talib found out about this evil conspiracy of the unbelievers of Quraysh, he gathered together all the people of his tribe and geared them up to exert all their energies in protecting the holy Prophet ﷺ. Consequently, Abu Talib took his beloved nephew and other members of his family, moved out of Makkah and camped in the Valley of Abu Talib (*shi'b Abi Talib*). Gradually other Muslims too began arriving there. Abu Talib was very cautious regarding the holy Prophet ﷺ, such that he would make a bed for the holy Prophet ﷺ in the evening and the holy Prophet ﷺ would rest on it for a while. When the other people would fall asleep, the caring and affectionate uncle would wake the holy Prophet ﷺ and take him to another location where another bed would be prepared on which the holy Prophet ﷺ would spend the night. Abu Talib would then get one of his sons to lie down on the first bed.

When the Quraysh realised that Abu Talib had taken his nephew and family with him and moved to the Valley of Abu Talib, all the tribes of Quraysh made preparations for a total social boycott. They would no longer have any social dealings and relationships with the Muslims. They would not purchase anything from them nor sell anything to them (until they would not hand the holy Prophet ﷺ over to them to be killed). When they had all agreed upon these terms and sanctions, they wrote them down in a document on parchment. Then they all solemnly declared to adhere to this social boycott, and they placed the parchment in the Ka'bah with great care, so that each person in Makkah would strongly abide by it.

From the seventh year following the announcement of prophethood to the tenth year, i.e. for three years, the holy Prophet Muhammad ﷺ along with his family suffered the hardships of a social boycott and living under siege. They lived under such harsh conditions that at times they had to eat leaves and grass to stay alive. But these difficult and testing conditions failed to weaken the resolve of the holy Prophet ﷺ and deter him from carrying out his duty as the Messenger of Almighty Allah.

One day the holy Prophet ﷺ said to his uncle Abu Talib that

the boycott agreement of the people which was hung up in the Ka'bah very carefully, all of its terms that were written had been eaten up by ants, except for wherever the name of *Allah* had been written. Abu Talib was very surprised to hear this from an individual sitting many miles away from Makkah under siege in a valley for three years, who is at this instance informing him of something that was very far, wrapped up in many covers, carefully kept inside the Ka'bah and which was continuously being guarded. Abu Talib asked: "Has your Lord told you this?" The holy Prophet ﷺ replied that indeed that was so, to which Abu Talib said: "Then you are telling the truth, for you have never said anything false."

Abu Talib along with a few other people went straight to the Ka'bah, called the Quraysh together and said: "Go and bring the boycott document out of the Ka'bah, perhaps we can come to some agreement between us and you." They got up quickly, went to the Ka'bah, brought out the agreement and placed it in front of everyone. Abu Talib said: "I have brought a very fair solution to you today. My nephew has told me, and he never lies, that this parchment that is with you has only the name of *Allah* written on it, everything else has been eaten by ants. Now you open it. If what my nephew has said is the truth, then we will not hand him to you under any circumstances, and if what he has said is not the truth, then we will give him up to you."

The unbelievers became very happy with this proposal of Abu Talib and accepted it, for they were confident that the conditions written on the parchment document would be undisturbed. They then opened the parchment up with their own hands, and found it to be exactly as the honest and truthful Messenger had said. Seeing this they were stunned and shocked, and burning in the fire of hatred and intolerance they said: "This is a trick of your nephew's magic!"

Truth had become clear as broad daylight, but the blind prejudice of the unbelievers of Makkah did not allow them to accept it. However, even in this unfair society there were some people who were increasingly becoming annoyed by the injustice and unfairness of the social boycott. One day a number of them went into the Ka'bah and ripped up the remaining pieces of parchment and declared the end of the boycott. So, in the tenth year following the announcement of prophethood, the holy Prophet ﷺ and his helpers gained freedom from this isolated confinement in the valley.

YEAR OF SORROW

It had not even been a month since freedom and return from the Valley of Abu Talib that Abu Talib passed away. A kind and affectionate uncle, who supported and stood by the holy Prophet ﷺ through thick and thin, was no longer alive. His departure was still fresh in the mind when a few days later the holy Prophet ﷺ faced another loss. His loyal life companion and beloved wife, Sayyidah Khadijah, also passed away. Both of these losses were great and painful tragedies for the holy Prophet Muhammad ﷺ and this is why this year is known as the Year of Sorrow (*'am al-huzn*).

Sayyidah Khadijah died at the age of sixty-five. She spent every moment of her twenty-five year marital life providing peace and comfort to the holy Prophet ﷺ, and she spent all of her wealth generously for the cause of Islam. There have been two individuals amongst the noble Companions who spent all of their wealth in the way of preaching and furthering the cause of Islam. Those two individuals are Sayyidah Khadijah and Abu Bakr al-Siddiq. Before embracing Islam, both of them were very rich and wealthy, and when they passed away they had next to nothing in terms of worldly goods with them.

Questions:

1. What did the leaders of Makkah think was the surest way of halting the spread of Islam?
2. What is *shi'b Abi Talib*, and why did the holy Prophet ﷺ move and camp there?
3. How many years did the holy Prophet Muhammad ﷺ remain in *shi'b Abi Talib*, and who else was with him?
4. What was the boycott, and how did it come about?
5. Describe the hardships faced by the holy Prophet ﷺ and the Muslims in *shi'b Abi Talib*?
6. Where was the boycott agreement of the Quraysh kept?
7. What was the holy Prophet's prophecy regarding the conditions written in the boycott agreement, and how did it come true?
8. What excuse did the Quraysh make for not honouring their agreement with Abu Talib?
9. What is the Year of Sorrow, and why is it called as such?

Chapter 16

Inviting the People of Ta'if

In the tenth year following the announcement of prophethood, when the holy Prophet Muhammad ﷺ continued to observe that the people of Makkah were becoming more severe day by day in their opposition to Islam, he took Zayd ibn Harithah with him and went to Ta'if. There he met the leaders of Ta'if and extended to them the message of Islam. But those unfortunate people responded negatively and turned against the holy Prophet ﷺ. They got a rowdy mob of their youngsters to go after the holy Prophet ﷺ and stone him. They began to throw stones at the holy Prophet ﷺ to the extent that his feet were injured causing them to bleed.

What would those terrible people know is the value of these blessed feet! Even the sandals (*na'layn*) worn on these feet are the coolness to the eyes of the people of love for the holy Prophet Muhammad ﷺ. It was the habit of 'Abdullah ibn Mas'ud that when the holy Prophet ﷺ would remove his sandals from his feet, he would pick the sandals up and hold them in his arms and when the holy Prophet ﷺ would require his sandals, 'Abdullah ibn Mas'ud would have the honour of putting the sandals on his blessed feet.

Upon leaving the town of Ta'if following this physical and mental torment, the holy Prophet Muhammad ﷺ entered an orchard and sat down under the shade of a grapevine. Having pity on the injured travellers, a worker in the orchard by the name of 'Addas offered a bunch of grapes. The holy Prophet ﷺ recited the name of Almighty Allah and then began to eat the grapes. 'Addas looked very carefully and closely at the enlightened face of the holy Prophet ﷺ and then said: "There is no tradition here of reciting Allah's name before eating." The holy Prophet ﷺ asked him: "What land are you from and what is your religion?" He replied: "I am a Christian and a citizen of Nineveh." The holy Prophet ﷺ responded: "That same Nineveh which is the land of the righteous Yunus ibn Matta (Jonah son of Matthew)?" 'Addas questioned: "How do you know about Yunus ibn Matta?"

"He is my brother, he was a Prophet and I am also a Prophet," replied the holy Prophet Muhammad ﷺ. 'Addas got up immediately and then respectfully kissed the holy Prophet's blessed forehead, then his hands and then began to kiss the blessed injured feet of the holy Prophet ﷺ.

After resting for a short time, the holy Prophet ﷺ began the journey back to Makkah. On the way, near the mountains, an angel appeared. After greeting the holy Prophet ﷺ, the angel informed him that he was sent by Almighty Allah to fulfil the instructions of the holy Prophet ﷺ. If the holy Prophet ﷺ so wished, he could crush the mountains together in such a way that the town of Ta'if and all its residents would be destroyed completely. But the embodiment of pure mercy, the holy Prophet Muhammad ﷺ, replied: "No! I am hopeful that Almighty Allah will create such offspring from their future generations who will become believers in the oneness of Almighty Allah."

Seeing this splendid mercy and affection of the holy Prophet Muhammad ﷺ, the angel spoke out: "Such has your Lord so named you. Indeed you are *ra'uf* (caring) and you are *rahim* (merciful)." It was as a result of the holy Prophet's mercy that the future generations of the people of Ta'if gained the blessings of Islam. If the holy Prophet ﷺ had taken revenge for the tyranny that was inflicted upon him, today there would be no sign of a place called Ta'if.

Moon Splits into Two

Once during a moonlit night, a group of polytheists of Makkah came to see the holy Prophet Muhammad ﷺ and said: "If you are a true Prophet then split the moon into two parts." The holy Prophet ﷺ replied: "If I split the moon into two, will you embrace Islam?" They all agreed that they would do so.

It was the night of a full moon. The beloved Messenger of Almighty Allah, the holy Prophet Muhammad ﷺ, pointed his finger towards the moon, and the moon split into two halves. The holy Prophet ﷺ began to call the names of each of the polytheists and said: "O so-and-so! See with your very own eyes, the moon has split into two." When the unbelievers witnessed this great miracle, they began to say that the holy Prophet ﷺ had cast a spell over their eyes through magic.

They further said that the caravans of travellers were due to arrive after a few days, and they would be asked about this incident. In this way, the reality of this magic would automatically become clear. On arrival, the caravans were asked whether they had observed the splitting of the moon on the particular night in question. They all confirmed seeing the moon amazingly split into two. But, in spite of this, the unbelievers of Makkah did not come into the folds of Islam.

Questions:

1. When did the holy Prophet ﷺ go to Ta'if?
2. What was the response of the people of Ta'if?
3. Who was 'Addas, and what was his encounter with the holy Prophet ﷺ?
4. What was the conversation between the angel and the holy Prophet ﷺ on the way back to Makkah?
5. What do you know about the splitting of the moon?
6. Who confirmed the splitting of the moon?

CHAPTER 17

NIGHT JOURNEY AND ASCENSION

A year before the holy Prophet Muhammad ﷺ emigrated to Madinah (Yathrib), on the 27th of the month of Rajab during a short span of the night, Almighty Allah granted his beloved last Prophet ﷺ a physical and spiritual journey to the heavens whilst he was in a wakeful state with body and soul. This blessed journey is divided into two parts. The first part consists of the journey from Makkah to Jerusalem and this is called the *isra'* (night journey). The second part of the journey consists of going from *Masjid Aqsa* (Al-Aqsa Mosque) in Jerusalem to the heavens and on to the furthest point (*sidrat al-muntaha*) and even far beyond that, and this part of the journey is called the *mi'raj* (ascension).

One night the holy Prophet Muhammad ﷺ was resting near the Ka'bah in the area called *hatim* (semi-circular area next to the wall of the Ka'bah originally part of it). The archangel Jibril (Gabriel) came and woke him up from his sleep, and then informed him of the intention of Almighty Allah. The holy

Prophet ﷺ got up and was taken near the well of Zamzam. There, his chest was opened up and his pure heart was filled with treasures of wisdom. The chest was then sealed up again. When the holy Prophet ﷺ came out of *Masjid Haram* (Sacred Mosque), an animal to ride on was presented called *buraq*. Its speed and stride was such that as far as its eyes could see, that is where the *buraq* would place its next step. The holy Prophet ﷺ rode on the back of this animal and travelled to Jerusalem. All of the previous Prophets of Almighty Allah were gathered together in Jerusalem and there they all performed prayer in *Masjid Aqsa* being led by the holy Prophet Muhammad ﷺ.

Afterwards, the journey to the heavens took place. The holy Prophet Muhammad ﷺ met different Prophets of Almighty Allah in various levels of the heavens. They then reached the furthest point (*sidrat al-muntaha*) where Jibril stopped and the holy Prophet ﷺ continued on further on his own beyond the furthest point. There, then Almighty Allah unveiled His divine essence and in that profoundly unexplainable seclusion, the holy Prophet ﷺ was granted awareness to such mysteries and communications, the exquisiteness and elegance of which are beyond the scope of words. The Qur'an has indicated towards this in the following verse:

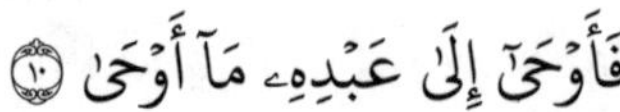

"So Allah revealed to His beloved servant what He revealed."
[*Qur'an* 53:10]

Among the special blessings received from this station of close proximity to Almighty Allah was the gift of fifty daily prayers, which upon the request of Prophet Musa (Moses [*as*]), the holy

Prophet Muhammad ﷺ asked for a reduction. Eventually the number of daily prayers was reduced to five, but the reward remained of fifty daily prayers. Prior to the *mi'raj*, the Muslims had been instructed to perform two daily prayers; one at dawn (*fajr*) and the other in the mid-afternoon (*'asr*).

The holy Prophet's journey to the heavens took place in a very short span of the night. In the morning, the holy Prophet ﷺ came next to the door of the Ka'bah and informed the people of Makkah that were present about the details of his journey to Jerusalem and the heavens. The unbelievers were shocked and responded by saying that whatever the holy Prophet ﷺ had been saying to them before was somewhat understandable, but what he was telling them now has shaken them to the core. How could they accept that the distance that could be covered in two months on a very fast camel, the holy Prophet ﷺ covered that same long distance in just a short period of time during one night?

The polytheists began to ask various questions so that they could succeed in disproving what the holy Prophet ﷺ was telling them. They knew very well that the holy Prophet ﷺ had not visited Jerusalem before. So they hurled many questions at the holy Prophet ﷺ about the architectural details of *Masjid Aqsa* in Jerusalem. How many doors does it have? What is the number of windows around it? What is its ceiling like? By His grace, Almighty Allah lifted the veils between the holy Prophet ﷺ and *Masjid Aqsa* and so he was able to see it in front of his eyes. As they continued to ask their questions, the holy Prophet ﷺ looked at *Masjid Aqsa* and answered them.

Questions:

1. What is meant by the night journey and ascension to the heavens, and how did it take place?
2. Where was the holy Prophet Muhammad ﷺ when the archangel Jibril came to him?
3. What are the two parts of this journey called?
4. What is the *buraq*, and how fast did it travel?
5. What gift did Almighty Allah give to the holy Prophet Muhammad ﷺ for the Muslims?
6. What happened the next morning when the holy Prophet ﷺ informed the people about his journey?

CHAPTER 18

ISLAM BEGINS IN YATHRIB

In order to take the people of Makkah out of their misfortune, the holy Prophet Muhammad ﷺ struggled tirelessly day and night for thirteen long years, but other than a small number of fortunate individuals, no one was able to accept Islam. When the days of the pilgrimage (*hajj*) would arrive, the majority of the tribes of Arabia would come to Makkah. During these times, the Messenger of mercy, the holy Prophet ﷺ, would go to the camps of each individual tribe and personally invite them towards Islam. But those blinded by their own intellects did not see the light of truth.

It is the eleventh year following the announcement of prophethood, and the season of the annual pilgrimage is fast approaching. From distant regions of the Arabian peninsula, people were arriving in Makkah to perform their pilgrimage. The holy Prophet Muhammad ﷺ like before began to go to the residences of each tribe, preached to them and invited them to accept Islam. One day the holy Prophet ﷺ reached the place of

'Aqabah and encountered a group of people from Yathrib. When the holy Prophet ﷺ invited them, they embraced the religion of Islam. This was a group of six people from the tribe of Khazraj, who upon gaining the blessings of Islam returned to Yathrib. There they began to preach and propagate Islam.

FIRST 'AQABAH ALLEGIANCE

The following year, i.e. the twelfth year following the announcement of prophethood, a group of twelve people from Yathrib headed for Makkah during the days of the pilgrimage. They had the opportunity to meet the holy Prophet Muhammad ﷺ at 'Aqabah where they pledged allegiance at the holy Prophet's hands of guidance affirming that they would not associate any partner with Almighty Allah, they would not steal or commit fornication or adultery, that they would not bury their daughters alive and kill their children, that they would not slander, and that they would honour the holy Prophet's instructions and commands. This pledge is known as the First 'Aqabah Allegiance (*bay'at 'aqabah ula*).

The holy Prophet Muhammad ﷺ sent Mus'ab ibn 'Umayr to Yathrib along with them when they returned, so that the propagation of Islam can be supported and increased. Mus'ab ibn 'Umayr preached Islam in such an effective and attractive manner that within a year, hundreds of people had embraced the religion of Islam.

When the people of Yathrib found out that their guide and leader, and their brothers in faith, were facing difficulties and persecution in Makkah, they all agreed that their delegation which was due to travel to Makkah during the next season of the pilgrimage, its members would insist and request the holy Prophet ﷺ to leave Makkah and come to them to Yathrib, thereby blessing their land with his sublime presence.

SECOND 'AQABAH ALLEGIANCE

During the season of the annual pilgrimage in the thirteenth year following the announcement of prophethood, the group led by Mus'ab ibn 'Umayr that departed from Yathrib heading for Makkah consisted of seventy such people who had accepted Islam. This group of Muslims met in secret with the holy Prophet Muhammad ﷺ in the valley of 'Aqabah and requested him to come to them in Yathrib. The people of Yathrib pledged allegiance to the holy Prophet ﷺ affirming that they would act according to the teachings of Islam and that they would give their lives to protect and defend him. This pledge is known as the Second 'Aqabah Allegiance (*bay'at 'aqabah thaniyah*).

When this group of Muslims returned back home to Yathrib, a new energy filled with enthusiasm and dedication was found in the movement of preaching and propagating Islam. The call of Islam began to resonate all around. The majority of the youth in Yathrib embraced Islam

Questions:

1. In the eleventh year after the announcement of prophethood, how many people from Yathrib entered

the folds of Islam?

2. What did the people from Yathrib pledge in the First 'Aqabah Allegiance?
3. Who did the holy Prophet Muhammad ﷺ send to Yathrib following the First 'Aqabah Allegiance, and why?
4. How many Muslims from Yathrib took part in the Second 'Aqabah Allegiance?
5. What did the Muslims of Yathrib pledge in the Second 'Aqabah Allegiance?

CHAPTER 19

THE EMIGRATION (HIJRAH)

The news that Islam was spreading in Yathrib and its people were becoming Muslim struck the people of Makkah like a flash of powerful lightning. They became even more hostile towards the Muslims and stepped up their campaign of oppression and tyranny against them. The holy Prophet Muhammad ﷺ then said to the noble Companions that whoever intends on emigrating should go to Yathrib. These sincere servants of Almighty Allah sacrificed their lands, their people, their homes, their courtyards, the wealth they had earned through hard work throughout their lives, and they pursued the *hijrah* (emigration) and left for Yathrib.

The mass emigration of Muslims caused confusion in the minds of the unbelievers of Makkah. They feared that if the holy Prophet ﷺ also leaves Makkah and goes to Yathrib, then it is quite possible that the Muslims might launch an attack on Makkah after some time. Before the situation spirals out of their control, they should take a decisive action. Hence a secret meeting of the leaders of Quraysh took place in *dar al-nadwah*. Satan (*shaytan*) too appeared there in human form wearing a silk garment, and he said: "I am a leader of Najd and I have come to give you better advice in how to solve this difficult situation." So, they allowed him to enter and join the meeting. When the actual discussion started, one of the leaders suggested that he should be chained and locked up until his life comes to an end. The leader of Najd responded by saying that when his devoted followers will find out, they will not hesitate in giving up their lives by coming to rescue him, so this suggestion is not worthy of being acted upon.

Further suggestions continued to be put forward. In the end, Abu Jahl said: "We should select a courageous young man from each tribe who is amongst the leaders of his tribe. Then each one of them should be armed with a sharp sword. Then they should all launch a sudden and ferocious attack, strike all together at once and kill him. The family of Banu Hashim would not be able to take revenge from all of the tribes and in the end would have to settle for financial compensation (blood money). We will very easily be able to pay that compensation money together." All of those who were in attendance agreed on this suggestion.

Eventually, on the chosen night, seven young men from the tribes of Quraysh including Abu Jahl armed with their swords stood outside the house in which the Beloved of Almighty Allah was residing. These cruel men were waiting for the moment that the holy Prophet ﷺ would step outside from his house, they would then all attack at once and kill him.

But look how astonishing this situation was that on the one

hand the people of Makkah were desperate to shed the blood of the holy Prophet ﷺ, yet on the other hand, they had given their own valuable goods and belongings to the holy Prophet ﷺ for safekeeping. In the history of mankind no example can be found whereby in a state of conflict the enemy is still trusted and depended upon. The world only witnessed this spectacle at the house of the Chosen One, the holy Prophet Muhammad ﷺ, whereby the enemy is coming and standing ready outside to take his life, yet inside he is making sure that their belongings and items given in trust are taken care of and duly safeguarded.

Inside the house, the holy Prophet ﷺ said to 'Ali that on this night he had been instructed to emigrate, and tonight 'Ali was to lie down in his bed covering himself with the holy Prophet's green sheet. He was not to worry, for no one would be able to harm him. The next day he was to return the valuable goods and belongings to their rightful owners. This was so that it becomes clear to everyone until the Day of Judgement that our beloved Prophet ﷺ was given the titles of *sadiq* (truthful) and *amin* (trustworthy) for the very reason that even in the most challenging, volatile and difficult moments, this is how he fulfilled the greatness of his character, integrity and trust.

After handing over the valuables and trusts of the people of Makkah to 'Ali, the holy Prophet Muhammad ﷺ stepped outside of his house and reciting the following verse from *Surat Ya-Sin*, he blew in the direction where the young men were waiting ready to spill his blood:

وَجَعَلْنَا مِنۢ بَيْنِ أَيْدِيهِمْ سَدًّا وَمِنْ خَلْفِهِمْ سَدًّا فَأَغْشَيْنَٰهُمْ فَهُمْ لَا يُبْصِرُونَ

"And We have set a barrier before them and a barrier behind them, and cast a veil over their eyes, so they see nothing." [*Qur'an* 36:9]

Consequently, all of those young men began to yawn and fall asleep. The holy Prophet ﷺ walked calmly through them and went to the house of Abu Bakr al-Siddiq. Taking Abu Bakr along with him, the holy Prophet ﷺ then left for the cave of Thawr, situated to the south of Makkah.

The night was dark and the route was through a difficult passage over rocky mountains. From time to time, Abu Bakr lifted the holy Prophet ﷺ up on to his shoulders across the hazardous terrain and kept a continuous look out to the left and to the right in case anyone was following them.

On reaching the opening of the cave, Abu Bakr requested: "Please wait out here. I will go inside first. If there is anything harmful, let it harm me first." Abu Bakr al-Sddiq entered the cave. The night was already dark and then this was a dark cave too, and nothing could be seen. He cleaned the cave and then checked every side and corner of the cave with his hands. Wherever he felt there was a hole, he plugged it with bits of cloth torn off from his cloak. But before all the holes were blocked, he ran out of pieces of cloth. There was one hole left that needed to be sealed. Abu Bakr sat down and placed his ankle against it, and then asked the holy Prophet ﷺ to come inside. The Beloved of Almighty Allah placed his blessed head in the lap of Abu Bakr and fell asleep.

There was a snake in the hole that Abu Bakr plugged with his ankle. During the night Abu Bakr was bitten several times, but he did not even startle and move an inch. He could not bear that the comfort and rest of the holy Prophet ﷺ be disrupted for any reason.

Meanwhile, dawn broke out in Makkah and the morning arrived. Instead of the holy Prophet ﷺ, it was 'Ali ibn Abi Talib who got out of the holy Prophet's bed. Witnessing this, those who had surrounded the house throughout the night were dumbfounded and could not work out how or when the holy Prophet ﷺ left his house. This news quickly spread to every house in Makkah. It was announced that whoever could capture the holy Prophet ﷺ and bring him back, dead or alive, will be given a reward of one hundred of the best red camels. Bounty hunters and groups of polytheists spread everywhere in search of the holy Prophet ﷺ.

A group of unbelievers reached the opening of the very cave in which the holy Prophet ﷺ and Abu Bakr were present. But Almighty Allah showed a sign of His power in such a way that a spider had covered the opening with a large and thick cobweb which appeared very old as if it had been there for a very long time undisturbed. In addition, two wild pigeons had made a nest at the opening of the cave and laid eggs in it.

When Abu Bakr saw the unbelievers standing outside, he said: "O Allah's Messenger! If they bend down and look, they will discover us." The holy Prophet Muhammad ﷺ replied: "O Abu Bakr! What do you think about those two, the third of whom is Almighty Allah? Do not worry, Almighty Allah is with us." One of the men standing outside the cave spoke out: "There is no need to enter this cave. The pigeon is sitting on its eggs and this cobweb is so old, it was probably here even before Muhammad's birth."

After spending three days in the cave, the holy Prophet ﷺ departed for Yathrib. On the way, someone approached them and asked Abu Bakr: "Who is this man with you?" Abu Bakr replied:

رَجُلٌ يَهْدِينِي الطَّرِيقَ

"This is a man who shows me the way!"

SURAQAH AND THE BRACELETS OF PERSIA

Suraqah was one of those men who set off from Makkah with the intention of capturing the holy Prophet Muhammad ﷺ in order to receive the reward of one hundred camels. He passed by the location from where the holy Prophet ﷺ was travelling. Having succeeded in sighting the holy Prophet ﷺ in front of him, he charged his horse full of joy. As he approached the holy Prophet ﷺ, his horse tripped and Suraqah fell to the ground. Suraqah remounted his horse and tried to gallop his horse once again. This time the horse sank into the ground up to its knees and Suraqah tumbled off the horse and fell on the ground. It was then that he became scared and realised that this was something else. Hence he pleaded for forgiveness and promised not to harm the holy Prophet ﷺ.

When Suraqah was about to go back, the holy Prophet Muhammad ﷺ said to him: "O Suraqah! What will be your glory on that day when you will be given the bracelets to wear of Chosroes, the King of Persia!"

Suraqah accepted Islam after the conquest of Makkah. During

the caliphate of 'Umar ibn al-Khattab, as the empire of Islam spread around the world, when the crown and the gold bracelets of Chosroes of Persia were presented to 'Umar, he gave the bracelets to Suraqah and put them on him. In this way, the promise of the holy Prophet ﷺ was fulfilled.

Arrival in Quba

When the people of Madinah (Yathrib) received the news that the holy Prophet Muhammad ﷺ had departed from Makkah, then everyday they would all gather in a plain ground outside Madinah to welcome and receive their leader and master, and they would remain waiting there all day until the sun would set. The next morning, they would hurry impatiently to the same place again in anticipation. At long last the wait was over and that moment finally came when the holy Prophet ﷺ could be seen coming from a distance from behind the mountains. The atmosphere of Madinah suddenly began to echo with welcome calls and chants. Muslims began to flock from every direction rushing in order to welcome and catch a glimpse of the holy Prophet ﷺ. They were greeting and congratulating each other, and they were expressing joy and happiness in many ways.

After departing from the cave of Thawr, it took the holy Prophet ﷺ twelve days to reach Quba. It was the twelfth of the month of Rabi' al-Awwal and the day was Monday. The holy Prophet ﷺ arrived at the moment the sun was about to decline from its zenith and was shining fiercely. Abu Bakr had taken his cloak off and was using it to provide shade to the holy Prophet ﷺ from the scorching heat, making it clear to the people who was the master and who was the servant.

EMIGRATION OF 'ALI

The mercy for the world, the holy Prophet Muhammad ﷺ, left his cousin brother 'Ali ibn Abi Talib in Makkah so that the properties that were given in trust to the holy Prophet ﷺ for safekeeping, he could return them to their rightful owners. It took 'Ali three days to fulfil this command and duty. He would stand in the middle of the square and invite people to take back the property they had left in trust with the holy Prophet Muhammad ﷺ.

After three days, 'Ali also departed from Makkah heading for Madinah. He undertook this journey on foot and walked so much over sandy hills and across mountainous regions that his blessed feet became swollen and started to bleed. When he eventually arrived in Quba, the holy Prophet ﷺ placed his blessed saliva over the injuries on his feet. The blessings of that were such that from that moment onwards until the end of his life with his martyrdom, 'Ali never suffered from any pain in his feet.

STAY IN QUBA

Quba was a small settlement close to Madinah. The holy Prophet Muhammad ﷺ stayed here for around two weeks. The first mosque to be built after the emigration (*hijrah*) was constructed here, which is called *Masjid Quba*. The holy Prophet ﷺ himself took part in this construction work. The holy Prophet ﷺ was carrying heavy stones himself and the dust from those stones was falling on to his pure body. A Companion would come forward and say: "Please do not burden yourself, allow me to carry this stone." The holy

Prophet ﷺ would reply: "Leave this one, you go and bring another stone like it."

When the construction of the mosque had been completed, the holy Prophet ﷺ stated: "The reward of performing one prayer in *Masjid Quba* is equal to the reward of performing one lesser pilgrimage (*'umrah*)."

Departure from Quba

The days the holy Prophet Muhammad ﷺ spent in Quba, the Muslims of Madinah would come morning and evening just to see the holy Prophet ﷺ and were restlessly waiting for the day when he would set foot in the city of Madinah. Eventually on the morning of one Friday, the holy Prophet ﷺ departed from Quba in a procession of Muslims. In the city of Madinah, preparations to welcome and receive the holy Prophet ﷺ were in full swing. Everyone was wearing their best clothes and adorned themselves with their armour. Groups of Abyssinians were joyously displaying their traditional martial skills. The holy Prophet Muhammad ﷺ was riding his camel and the Muslims were cheerfully reciting the following call:

اَللّٰهُ اَكْبَرُ جَاءَ رَسُولُ اللّٰهِ . اَللّٰهُ اَكْبَرُ جَاءَ مُحَمَّدٌ

"Allah is the Greatest, Allah's Messenger has arrived!
Allah is the Greatest, Muhammad ﷺ has arrived!"

The land of Yathrib resonated with chants of the oneness (*tawhid*) of Almighty Allah and the messengership (*risalah*) of His Beloved ﷺ. The whole area was packed full of people and there was no space left in the streets. The surrounding houses and the rooftops were filled with people anxious to catch a glimpse of the holy Prophet ﷺ. Young girls of Madinah were playing the *daff* and were welcoming their beloved guest by singing the following verses:

طَلَعَ الْبَدْرُ عَلَيْنَا . مِنْ ثَنِيَّاتِ الْوَدَاع

وَجَبَ الشُّكْرُ عَلَيْنَا . مَا دَعَا لِلّٰهِ دَاع

أَيُّهَا الْمَبْعُوثُ فِينَا . جِئْتَ بِالْأَمْرِ الْمُطَاع

"The full moon has arisen, from the valley of Wada';
As long as the call is for Allah, we must show gratefulness.
O the one who has come to us as a Prophet;
You have come with a word to be obeyed."

Quite some time had passed since this procession had begun, yet only a short distance had been covered. When the procession reached the locality of Banu Salim, the sun had declined from its zenith and the time had started to perform the Friday Prayer. The instruction was given to offer the Friday Prayer there in an open ground. Within a few minutes the noble Companions had straightened their rows and with utmost respect sat down waiting for the prayer. This was the first Friday Prayer which the people of Yathrib performed in the leadership of the holy Prophet ﷺ, and this was the first Friday Sermon which the holy Prophet ﷺ delivered in the newly found freedom offered by the Yathrib atmosphere. In his sermon, the holy Prophet Muhammad ﷺ glorified Almighty Allah and then encouraged the people to pursue the way of righteousness and to better their hereafter.

After completing the Friday Prayer, the holy Prophet ﷺ again mounted his camel and continued along. Whichever locality he would pass by, its leader would come forward and request that the holy Prophet ﷺ stays with them and grants them the honour of hosting him. The holy Prophet ﷺ rested the camel's reins on her neck and said: "Clear the way for my camel. Almighty Allah has given her the instruction. The camel will stop according to the command of Almighty Allah."

When the procession reached the locality of the Banu Najjar, the camel suddenly sat down in an open ground. The closest house to the camel was that of Abu Ayyub al-Ansari who came forward and took the luggage of the holy Prophet ﷺ to his house. In this way, the house that Almighty Allah selected for the residence of His Beloved was not the palaces of leaders, rather it was a simple and ordinary house of a very simple and down to earth servant.

Abu Ayyub relates that they used to prepare the food and send it to the holy Prophet Muhammad ﷺ. When the cutlery and the food would be returned, they used to look for the signs and imprints of the holy Prophet's blessed fingers, and where they used to find them, they would eat from there in order to gain blessings (*barakah*).

Questions:

1. What were the leaders of Makkah worried about when they found out that Islam was spreading in Yathrib?

2. What did the leaders of Makkah decide to do about the holy Prophet ﷺ when they met in *dar al-nadwah*?
3. What did the holy prophet ﷺ do after he left his house on the night he migrated to Yathrib?
4. What did the holy Prophet ﷺ ask 'Ali to do?
5. Why could the seven assassins waiting outside the holy Prophet's house not see him leaving the house?
6. On reaching the cave of Thawr, what did Abu Bakr do, and what happened to him during the night?
7. What reward did the leaders of Makkah decide to offer to anyone who could capture the holy Prophet ﷺ?
8. Who was Suraqah, and what happened to him?
9. What did the holy Prophet ﷺ say to Suraqah about what was to happen to him in the future?
10. Describe the scene as the holy Prophet Muhammad ﷺ and Abu Bakr al-Siddiq arrived in Quba.
11. When did 'Ali ibn Abi Talib leave Makkah heading for Madinah?
12. How long did the holy Prophet ﷺ stay in Quba?
13. Where was the first mosque built after emigrating to Madinah, and what was it called?
14. How did the Muslims in Madinah celebrate the arrival of the holy Prophet Muhammad ﷺ?
15. Where did the holy Prophet ﷺ perform the first congregational prayer of Friday?
16. How did the holy Prophet ﷺ decide where he was going to stay in Madinah?
17. Where and with whom did the holy Prophet ﷺ stay?

CHAPTER 20

BUILDING THE PROPHET'S MOSQUE

The area close to the house of Abu Ayyub al-Ansari where the holy Prophet Muhammad's camel had sat down on the first day, the holy Prophet ﷺ selected this area for a mosque. This land was owned by two orphan children named Sahl and Suhayl. The holy Prophet ﷺ called the two orphans and discussed with them the purchasing of this land. Both Sahl and Suhayl stated that they will present this portion of land as a gift to the holy Prophet ﷺ. But the holy Prophet ﷺ refused to accept this land free of charge. Consequently, the portion of land was valued at ten *dinars* (gold coins) and this amount was paid by Abu Bakr al-Siddiq.

After purchasing this land, work began on constructing a mosque on it, which became *Masjid Nabawi* (Prophet's Mosque). The holy Prophet ﷺ took an active part in this building work alongside his Companions. On one occasion, the holy Prophet ﷺ was carrying a stone for the mosque when a Companion stepped forward and asked that the holy

Prophet ﷺ give the stone to him to carry. The holy Prophet ﷺ replied: "Go and get another stone. You are not more in need of Allah's mercy than me."

During this construction work, the noble Companions were all carrying one stone each and bringing it to the construction site. However, another Companion 'Ammar would be carrying two stones; one for himself and one for the holy Prophet ﷺ. When the holy Prophet ﷺ saw him, he stroked his back affectionately and said: "O 'Ammar! People will gain one measure of reward, but you will gain two measures of reward. And you will be martyred by a rebellious group."

After the building of the mosque, the holy Prophet ﷺ began the construction of living quarters for his wives. But these were not built all in one go, rather as the need arose, the living quarters were extended and constructed. After the holy Prophet ﷺ when his pure wives had passed away, these living quarters became part of the Prophet's Mosque.

Questions:

1. Who originally owned the land on which *Masjid Nabawi* was built?
2. Who paid for the purchase of this land?
3. Describe the holy Prophet's role in the construction of *Masjid Nabawi*.

CHAPTER 21

UNIQUE BROTHERHOOD

The people of Madinah who embraced Islam were not members of one tribe only, rather they belonged to different tribes and families. These tribes had been fighting wars and battles against one another for centuries. Seeds of conflict and dispute were also present in the people who had emigrated from Makkah too. In order to make unity amongst the people more firm and to strengthen it as well as to settle those who had emigrated to Madinah with dignity, the holy Prophet Muhammad ﷺ established a unique system of brotherhood between the *muhajirun* (emigrants) who came from Makkah and the *ansar* (helpers) who were residents of Madinah. The holy Prophet ﷺ declared one emigrant to be a brother to one helper and in this way each person from the *muhajirun* found a brother amongst the *ansar*, so that they could live their lives assisting and helping one another. The *ansar* demonstrated such great examples of sacrifice and selflessness for their emigrant brothers that no nation of the world can show to have anything like this brotherhood.

One day the *ansar* came to the holy Prophet ﷺ with a request and asked: "O Allah's Messenger! Divide our lands and distribute it equally between us and our emigrant brothers." The holy Prophet ﷺ did not accept this request and said: "They will share in the fruits and produce of the land, but not the ownership of the land."

When 'Abd al-Rahman ibn 'Awf emigrated and arrived in Madinah, the holy Prophet Muhammad ﷺ established a bond of brotherhood declaring him to be a brother to Sa'd ibn al-Rabi' al-Ansari. Sa'd turned to his new Islamic brother 'Abd al-Rahman and said: "You are my brother. I am the wealthiest person amongst the people of Madinah. You can halve everything that belongs to me. One half you can take and the other half you can leave for me. I am also prepared to divorce one of my two wives so she can marry you with her consent, if you so wish." 'Abd al-Rahman ibn 'Awf was very impressed and greatly affected by this kindness and selflessness demonstrated by his brother, but declined the offer and said: "O my brother! May Almighty Allah bless your wealth and your wives and family in abundance. You just show me the way to the trade market." Eventually he began a trading business and after some time, his business became so successful that hundreds of camels carrying the trading goods of 'Abd al-Rahman ibn 'Awf would go to various markets.

This society of Madinah that came into existence due to the practical wisdom of the holy Prophet Muhammad ﷺ consisted of two fundamental elements. One was the *ansar*, who were embodiments of sincerity and selfless generosity and who presented half of their lands, properties and everything they owned with full heartfelt sincerity. The other was the dignified *muhajirun*, who did not wish to become a burden on their kind hosts and wanted to earn a lawful livelihood themselves through their own hard work and dedication. Both of these groups of people were unique and matchless in their own right and both were a result of the blessings of the Chosen One, the holy Prophet Muhammad ﷺ, which turned them into these timeless symbols of love, determination and gratitude.

Questions:

1. What steps did the holy Prophet Muhammad ﷺ take in Madinah to establish unity among the Muslims?
2. Who are the *ansar*?
3. Who are the *muhajirun*?
4. Give one example to show the generosity and sincerity of the *ansar* towards the *muhajirun*?

CHAPTER 22

CONSTITUTION OF MADINAH

Other than the Muslims, there was also a powerful community of various Jewish tribes who lived in Madinah. They were economically prosperous and affluent, and they also had superiority amongst the people of Madinah in terms of knowledge and they occupied the moral and educational high ground, since they were recipients of the previous heavenly book. Full unity and peace in the society here could not be established until the Jews were not involved. Furthermore, the original enemies of Islam, the people of Makkah, were still adamant on putting an end to the Muslims and at any moment they could launch an attack on Madinah. In order to address these internal and external threats and difficulties, a broad and wide-ranging charter was needed.

In view of this, the holy Prophet Muhammad ﷺ devised a comprehensively written treaty which included the Jews as well as the *muhajirun* (emigrants) and the *ansar* (helpers) of the Muslims. By virtue of this treaty, practical unity and peace were established amongst all of the inhabitants of Madinah irrespective of their religious and ethnic background, and the internal and external challenges, threats and needs were all addressed.

This treaty was the world's first written constitution, which became known as the *Constitution of Madinah.* Some of its terms are summarised as follows:

1. All Muslims will collectively oppose any individual who transgresses and pursues the path of oppression and tyranny towards anyone else. In opposition to such a person, all Muslims will stand united even if the oppressor is one of their own sons.

2. Anyone from the Jewish community who cooperates with the Muslims will be provided with assistance and will be treated equally as Muslims. They will not be harmed and the Muslims will not aid their enemy too.

3. Any person who is found guilty of murder, he will be given the death penalty in retaliation (*qisas*), unless the victim's relative forgives the murderer and agrees to a financial compensation.

4. When a dispute and disagreement occurs between any Muslims, the matter will be presented before Almighty Allah and His Messenger Muhammad ﷺ.

5. The Jews will be considered as one group with the Muslims. The Jews reserve the right to practise and follow their own religion and the Muslims will practise

and adhere to their own religion. However, those guilty of tyranny or breaking the agreement will only harm themselves.

6. If war is waged against the adherers to this treaty and they are attacked, then all parties including the Muslims and the Jews will help one another collectively. In addition, all groups will remain sincere in their well-wishes and dealings with one another. Their pride will be their loyalty to each other, and not disloyalty and the breaking of pledges. Every individual suffering cruelty and oppression will be helped.

7. A refugee and anyone seeking protection will be like the one who is protected by the constitution. No one is to harm the refugee, and he is not to break the agreement too.

8. Whoever attacks the city of Madinah, then everyone including the Muslims and the Jews will take up arms to confront the aggressors and will help one another. As long as a battle and armed conflict continues with any enemy, each group, Muslims and Jews, will cover their own individual military expenditure.

Questions:

1. What steps did the holy Prophet Muhammad ﷺ take in order to unite all the people living in Madinah?

2. List four important points from the constitution that the holy Prophet ﷺ devised for the people of Madinah.

CHAPTER 23

MILITARY EXPEDITIONS

In the books of prophetic biography (*sirah*), the military expeditions that took place during the life of the holy Prophet Muhammad ﷺ, irrespective of whether fighting occurred in them and they turned into battles or no fighting occurred and they remained as mere campaigns, are referred to as *ghazawat* (singular: *ghazwah*).

A *ghazwah* is the expedition in which the holy Prophet ﷺ personally participated and travelled with. A *sariyyah* is a cavalry unit in which the holy Prophet ﷺ did not himself participate, but he did despatch it by appointing a Companion of his to lead and command it.

ARMED JIHAD IS PERMITTED

Since the beginning of the preaching of Islam, for over thirteen years, the unbelievers of Makkah continuously persecuted the Muslims in numerous cruel and brutal ways, and they made life so difficult for them that eventually they were forced to leave everything behind in Makkah and live in a state of exile four hundred and sixty-five kilometres away, in Madinah. But even there, far away in Madinah, the unbelievers did not allow them to live in peace.

Consequently, Almighty Allah granted the long-suffering, oppressed and patient Muslim community permission to fight in their self-defence and pursue armed *jihad* (struggle), i.e. they could now respond to force with force, but with strict and specific conditions.

They were not allowed to take up arms for theft and banditry, nor for settling personal grudges and scores, and nor for gaining business expediency. They were only permitted to struggle in order to uphold the truth and only against those who waged war against them or were preparing to attack them. They were granted this permission with the firm and uncompromising condition that no one would be oppressed and transgressed against, i.e. they could not harm nor raise their hands against women, children, elderly, farmers, labourers, religious leaders, and they were even not allowed to destroy crops in the lands, trees and green fields.

In the present developed and sophisticated world, is there any nation in existence whose rules of military conflict provide such safeguarding measures and give such consideration to justice and fairness to this profound level? Today, as soon as war breaks out peaceful citizens and populated civilian settlements are completely destroyed through bombardment and a barrage of bombs and explosions. Women, innocent children, elderly, and even the sick are not spared. Hospitals, educational establishments and places of worship are all not given any respect.

Questions:

1. What is the difference between *ghazwah* and *sariyyah*?
2. For how long did the holy Prophet Muhammad ﷺ propagate Islam in Makkah?
3. What is meant by *jihad*?
4. In relation to its purpose, what conditions did Almighty Allah impose on Muslims during armed *jihad*?
5. What are the Muslims not allowed to do during *jihad*?
6. How are the wars of today different?

CHAPTER 24

BATTLE OF BADR

The people of Makkah had forcefully occupied the houses and properties of the Muslims who had emigrated from Makkah and took over their lands. Further, they began to threaten the Jews of Madinah and demanded that they force the Muslims out of Madinah. In order to intimidate the Muslims and show their strength and power over them, they sent a party of raiders and looters which attacked and ransacked an area of Madinah used for grazing animals. They killed the shepherd and marched the herd of goats and camels to Makkah. This successful attack and raid from their part raised the nerve of the unbelievers of Makkah and they become bolder. So, they formally began making preparations to launch an outright attack on the city of Madinah.

The leaders of Makkah despatched a unique and exceptional trade caravan to Syria under the leadership of Abu Sufyan, so that they could finance and cover the cost and expenses of their imminent attack on Madinah from the income generated by this trade caravan. When this caravan was on its way back returning from Syria, the holy Prophet Muhammad ﷺ invited the Muslims to go in its pursuit. Hence the holy Prophet ﷺ accompanied by three hundred and thirteen of his selfless Companions departed from Madinah.

The Muslims had only one horse and eighty camels to ride on, and the rest of the soldiers walked on foot. The holy Prophet ﷺ appointed each camel to a group of three or four of the Companions who would ride the camel in turn. When the holy Prophet Muhammad ﷺ had covered the distance of his turn, he dismounted from the camel so that the other person could ride on it. Both of his Companions spoke out: "O Allah's Messenger! Please continue to ride the camel even when it is our turn." The holy Prophet ﷺ replied: "Neither of you is stronger than me, nor is it the case that I am not in need of reward and only you are in need of it."

When Abu Sufyan received the news that the holy Prophet ﷺ had left the city of Madinah and was on his way in his pursuit, he sent an urgent message to Makkah that they should immediately come to his aid. The unbelievers of Makkah were stirred into action by this message and each person began to get ready to fight against the Muslims. Consequently, a large army of the unbelievers of Makkah consisting of one thousand soldiers set off from Makkah being led by Abu Jahl. They had one hundred horses, six hundred camels, a troupe of slave girls to sing and dance, and an ample amount of weapons and military gear with them. Meanwhile, Abu Sufyan's caravan had passed by before the Muslims had arrived and it reached an area where it could not be confronted by the Muslims. He sent another message to the people of Makkah that his caravan was now safe, so there was no need to continue the march and fight the Muslims, for now. However, Abu Jahl refused to turn back to Makkah and boasted that they would continue on and teach the Muslims a bitter lesson at the place of Badr.

Soon, the holy Prophet ﷺ received news that Abu Sufyan's caravan had managed to move along swiftly and was out of reach, but the Quraysh of Makkah were steadily marching towards them with a large military force. So, the holy Prophet ﷺ consulted with his Companions in view of this latest development and changing situation on the ground. The noble Companions replied: "O Allah's Messenger! Go wherever you decide, we will go with you. If you give us a signal to dive into the ocean or face up to the enemy, we will happily and anxiously sacrifice our lives. We are hopeful that Almighty Allah will enable us to demonstrate such a feat for you which will bring coolness to your eyes. So, please proceed with the blessing of Almighty Allah. We will not give you the answer that the Israelites gave to Prophet Musa (Moses [*as*]), when they said to him that he and his Lord should go and fight the enemy, but they were not prepared to fight and would remain behind in comfort. Rather, we will say to you that please continue forward, let us march with you and your Lord into battle with the enemy."

Hearing their passionate sentiments, the holy Prophet ﷺ was pleased and then he said to them: "I can see exactly where the unbelievers will fall tomorrow in the battleground." So, the holy Prophet ﷺ continued on his journey heading towards Badr with his dedicated Companions and they reached the plain of Badr before the unbelievers had arrived. The plain of Badr is located around eighty miles from Madinah.

It is the day of Friday, 17th of Ramadan. On one side there is a strong army of one thousand unbelievers with extensive weaponry and military gear, and on the other side there are three hundred and thirteen Muslims with a small number of swords and spears. The holy Prophet ﷺ held an arrow in his hand and was straightening the rows into battle formation. Any soldier who would be a step forward or backward from his line, the holy Prophet ﷺ would point with his arrow to straighten the row and not allow the formation to be broken. The holy Prophet ﷺ was walking in front of one of the rows and saw that Sawad was standing one step forward from his row (perhaps he moved forward to kiss the holy Prophet's hands). The holy Prophet ﷺ lightly pressed with his arrow on his stomach and said: "O Sawad! Straighten yourself!"

Sawad straightened himself but then immediately said: "O Allah's Messenger! I have been hurt by this. So let me get even?" The flagbearer of justice and fairness, the holy Prophet ﷺ, did not take this request as disrespect or as an insult. A mere soldier whilst standing on the battleground demanding something like this from the commander-in-chief, for this he was not punished or ordered to be court-martialled. Rather, without displaying even a small sign of disappointment, the holy Prophet ﷺ lifted up his garment, presented his blessed stomach and said: "O Sawad! Come and take your revenge." Sawad immediately leaped forward, embraced the holy Prophet ﷺ and kissed his stomach. The holy Prophet ﷺ asked: "Sawad! Why did you do this?" He replied: "O Allah's Messenger! You are well aware of the situation that lies in front of us. It was my deep wish that before I die in battle, my skin touches your blessed skin." The holy Prophet ﷺ displayed his contentment at this wish and prayed for Sawad.

Battle Commences

When the two armies came face to face, three men from the unbelievers stepped forward, namely 'Utbah, Shaybah and Walid, and they challenged the Muslims to combat. So, the holy Prophet Muhammad ﷺ sent forward Hamzah, 'Ali and 'Ubaydah to go and face them. With their swords, Hamzah defeated and killed Shaybah, and 'Ali defeated and killed Walid. 'Utbah was also killed, but 'Ubaydah, however, was severely injured and succumbing to his injuries, he died placing his head on the feet of the holy Prophet ﷺ. Before he died, the holy Prophet ﷺ gave him the glad tidings of achieving martyrdom.

After this one to one combat, the two armies clashed with each other and a full scale battle broke out. For a short while, the holy Prophet ﷺ went back to his command centre (*'arish*), which was the spot where the Muslims had constructed a shade for the holy Prophet ﷺ at Badr. With great humbleness and profound humility, the holy Prophet ﷺ raised his hands in prayer and supplicated: "O Allah! Fulfil Your true promise. If these unbelievers overpower the Muslims today, then *shirk* (polytheism) will dominate, and then Your religion will not be established." After praying to his Lord, the holy Prophet ﷺ returned to the battleground, picked up a handful of pebbles and threw them in the direction of the unbelievers. With his sword in his hand, the holy Prophet ﷺ moved forward and began to confront the enemy in battle.

In order to help the Muslims, Almighty Allah sent down thousands of angels. The noble Companions stated: "At times when we would leap forward with our swords to strike the enemy, we would see that before our swords touched the enemy, his head would be chopped and fall to the ground." Clearly, this was the effect of divine help from the unseen (*ghayb*). As soon as the holy Prophet ﷺ joined in the fighting, the face of the battleground changed and the balance of power was overturned. Experiencing defeat, the polytheists began to retreat and flee from the battleground. Seventy unbelievers were killed in this battle including Abu Jahl and seventy were taken as prisoners of war. The number of Muslims who were martyred was only fourteen.

In this battle, the arm of Mu'adh had been almost completely chopped off, hanging barely from the shoulder. He came in the lofty presence of the holy Prophet Muhammad ﷺ, who placed his blessed saliva on his wound. The wound was miraculously healed and the arm completely cured and joined back to his shoulder.

In this battle also, the sword of 'Ukashah broke into two pieces, so the holy Prophet ﷺ gave him a dry branch of a tree and told him to fight with it. When 'Ukashah took hold of that branch and moved it a bit in his hand, it turned into a white metal sword. Even in the battles after this during his life, 'Ukashah fought using this same miraculous sword.

It was also in this same battle that Qatadah was severely injured with an arrow piercing through his eye, such that his eye was dislodged and began to droop down his cheek. The holy Prophet ﷺ called Qatadah and with his blessed hands wiped his cheek, placed his oozing eye back and put his hand over it. His eye was miraculously healed such that Qatadah could no longer tell which one of his eyes was injured.

A day before the battle, the leader of both worlds, the holy Prophet Muhammad ﷺ, had inspected the battlefield. As the holy Prophet ﷺ would walk passed a certain spot, he would point out that the dead body of so-and-so would be lying here. 'Umar al-Faruq said: "By the One who sent our Prophet with the truth! The dead bodies of the unbelievers were not even a little bit away from the place where the holy Prophet ﷺ had pointed out they would be."

Although these people were the worst enemies of Islam, nevertheless, the holy Prophet Muhammad ﷺ did not tolerate that their dead bodies remain outside in the open desert to be eaten by wild beasts and birds of prey. Instead, the dead bodies were all buried underground in a disused well and covered up with soil.

The holy Prophet ﷺ camped in Badr for a further three days, after which when he was about to depart for Madinah, he came to that well where the unbelievers had been buried. He stood near the mass grave and called out: "O unbelievers of Quraysh! If you had obeyed me then you would not be in your present state of plight. You were very cruel relatives. You forced me out of my home, rejecting me. Other people gave me refuge, believing in me."

Hearing this, 'Umar said: "O Allah's Messenger! Three days have passed since they died and today you are calling out to them. How can bodies void of souls hear?" The holy Prophet ﷺ replied: "You are not hearing what I am saying more clearer than they are. They are now listening to what I am saying, but they are not able to answer. In fact, they are now convinced that what I was telling them was the truth."

Prisoners of War

After the battle, the holy Prophet ﷺ called a meeting to consult about the seventy prisoners of war that had been captured during the battle. Several suggestions were put forward including that these oppressors be given the death penalty. The suggestion which the Prophet of mercy, the holy Prophet Muhammad ﷺ, preferred was that each prisoner should be set free in return for a financial ransom according to whatever amount the prisoner could afford, and whosoever from amongst the prisoners could not afford to pay any ransom, he should teach ten children of Madinah to read and write, and he would be set free.

In order to be set free, four hundred *dirhams* (silver coins) were demanded as ransom from 'Abbas, who replied that he does not have that much wealth and so could not afford to pay this amount of ransom. The holy Prophet ﷺ stated: "Dear uncle! What has happened to the wealth and possessions that you and my aunt Umm al-Fadl together buried in the ground, and you told my aunt that if you were to die in battle then she was to give that wealth to your children?" On hearing this, the eyes of 'Abbas opened and he saw the reality. He responded: "Today I have realised and become aware that you are indeed the true Messenger of Almighty Allah, because no one had knowledge of this matter other than me and Umm al-Fadl."

Questions:

1. What did the unbelievers of Makkah tell the Jews of

Madinah to do to the Muslims?

2. What did the raiders from Makkah do in Madinah?
3. How did the leaders of Makkah plan to finance their attack on the Muslims, and what was the role of Abu Sufyan in this preparation?
4. What did Abu Sufyan do when he realised that the Muslims were following his caravan?
5. How did the people of Makkah respond to Abu Sufyan's call for help?
6. What did Abu Jahl decide when the army from Makkah received Abu Sufyan's second message that no help was needed?
7. In the Battle of Badr, what was the strength of the army of unbelievers and the strength of the Muslims?
8. Where did the Battle of Badr take place?
9. Describe the incident involving Sawad.
10. Name those Muslims who took part in the one to one combat at the start of the battle.
11. In what form did divine help come to the Muslims?
12. How many unbelievers were killed in this battle and how many were taken as prisoners of war?
13. How many Muslims were martyred in this battle?
14. What did the holy Prophet ﷺ decide to do with the prisoners of war?
15. Describe how the holy Prophet's uncle 'Abbas accepted the religion of Islam.

CHAPTER 25

BATTLE OF UHUD

After experiencing defeat in the Battle of Badr, the people of Makkah were greatly distressed and took this defeat very badly. They immediately began making preparations for revenge. Together with brave men from other tribes in the surrounding areas, they gathered a large fighting force and, in the third year after the emigration (*hijrah*), they marched towards Madinah. Their army this time consisted of three thousand soldiers, and they had two hundred horses and three thousand camels with them.

When the Jews and the hypocrites of Madinah heard that the unbelievers of Quraysh were coming to attack the Muslims with a very large and fearsome army, they became very happy and rejoiced. This army of the unbelievers camped a few miles from Madinah on the foothills of Mount Uhud.

The holy Prophet ﷺ set off from Madinah with one thousand men, but on the way three hundred hypocrites deserted the

Muslims and returned home, and so with seven hundred selfless and devoted followers the holy Prophet Muhammad ﷺ continued on and confronted the unbelievers at Uhud. Behind the Muslims there was a hillock with a pass through which the enemy could strike from the rear. Therefore, the holy Prophet ﷺ stationed fifty archers near the pass on the high ground of this hillock led by 'Abdullah ibn Jubayr. The holy Prophet ﷺ gave them an emphatic command saying: "If we are victorious, even then you are to remain steadfast and stay in your positions, so that the enemy cannot attack us from your side. And if you see that the enemy has the upper hand and is overwhelming us, even then you are not to come to our aid, unless I send a specific message to you. Hear me clearly! As long as you remain in your positions, we shall prevail."

The battle commenced and the two armies began to fight each other bravely. The flag of Islam was in the hand of Mus'ab ibn 'Umayr. In order to cause the flag of Islam to fall, the unbelievers attacked him and his right hand was slashed. Mus'ab raised the flag high in his left hand. When the enemy cut his left hand too, he held the flag with both of his slashed arms, until he was martyred. Then the holy Prophet ﷺ passed the flag of Islam to 'Ali ibn Abi Talib.

The Muslims fought with such courage, passion and self-sacrifice that the unbelievers lost their footing and began to flee from the battleground. The Muslims began to gather the equipment and possessions left behind by the fleeing enemy. The archers who were stationed on the high ground guarding the pass behind the Muslim army assumed that victory had been achieved and there was no point in standing there any longer, rather they ought to go on to the battleground and join in collecting the spoils of war along with their comrades. Forty of the archers left their positions and came to the battleground despite 'Abdullah ibn Jubayr telling them not to. This hurried action of theirs turned the victory of Islam into defeat. As soon as the archers had left their posts, the enemy was quick to martyr the remaining ten archers and then attacked the Muslim army from the rear through the pass in such a swift manner that the course of the battle changed and now the Muslims lost their foothold.

The unbelievers tried to find a way to kill the holy Prophet Muhammad ﷺ, but the holy Prophet ﷺ was firing arrows at the enemy with his Companions. In the heat of this moment, the holy Prophet's forehead was injured, his lips bled and his front teeth were broken. During this intense fighting, someone shouted that the holy Prophet ﷺ had been killed. Hearing this the Muslims were further disheartened and some faint-hearted Muslims fled the battleground and returned to Madinah. But there were those courageous ones too who were increasing passion and resolve, shouting out: "Carry on and continue fighting! The religion for which our Prophet ﷺ has been martyred, we will give our heads too in order to raise high its flag. There is no point staying alive after the holy Prophet ﷺ!" Just then, someone shouted that the holy Prophet Muhammad ﷺ was alive and present there in front of them. When the Muslims heard this, they all immediately came together and regrouped themselves. Those who were spread out returned to the battleground, but by then the battle was over.

Seventy Muslims were martyred in this battle. When the battle had ended, both armies separated. The unbelievers mutilated the bodies of the Muslims martyred at Uhud, cutting off body parts such as the ears and nose (in a ritual known as *muthlah*). The body of the holy Prophet's martyred uncle, Hamzah, was cut open, his liver taken out and chewed on. These actions distressed the Muslims, but the holy Prophet ﷺ prohibited the *muthlah* of dead bodies and did not allow the Muslims to mutilate and mistreat the dead bodies of even their enemies. When the army of the unbelievers had left, the holy Prophet ﷺ buried the martyrs at Uhud and returned to Madinah. The holy Prophet Muhammad ﷺ would regularly come and visit these graves of the martyrs at Uhud, and he said: "Those who will come to visit them or will send them greetings of peace (*salam*) until the Day of Judgement, they will continue to respond to those salutations."

The defeat of the Muslims in the Battle of Uhud raised the confidence of the Jews and the hypocrites in Madinah. They became bolder and began to betray the treaty and agreement they had with the Muslims. They even went further and conspired to murder the holy Prophet Muhammad ﷺ. Upon this, in the fourth year after the emigration (*hijrah*), the holy Prophet ﷺ sent a message to the Jewish tribes who were part of this betrayal and plot instructing them to leave his city of Madinah. They were given ten days in which they should leave; if they remained in Madinah after these ten days, the Muslims would confront them due to their violation of the terms of the treaty and their conspiracies. The Jews rejected this call and refused to leave, upon which the holy Prophet ﷺ and the Muslims surrounded them to confront them for their wrongdoings. Eventually, when they were unable to face the Muslims, the Jews left and emigrated from Madinah.

Questions:

1. What was the number of Muslims and the unbelievers in the Battle of Uhud?
2. Where did this battle take place?
3. What did the holy Prophet Muhammad ﷺ instruct the fifty archers, and who commanded this group?
4. Describe the bravery of Mus'ab ibn 'Umayr in this battle.
5. When the unbelievers started to run away from the battleground, what did forty of the archers do?
6. What rumour did the enemy spread during this battle, and how did the Muslims react?
7. What injury did the holy Prophet ﷺ sustain during this battle?
8. How did the unbelievers and the Muslims treat the dead bodies of their opponents?
9. What did the holy Prophet ﷺ say regarding the graves of the martyrs of Uhud?
10. What led to some of the Jewish tribes leaving the city of Madinah?

CHAPTER 26

BATTLE OF THE TRENCH

The Quraysh of Makkah and the polytheist tribes of Arabia soon came to the conclusion that they could not defeat the Muslims on their own through their individual campaigns. Hence in the fifth year after the emigration (*hijrah*), they were able to unite together all of the groups and factions that were opposed to Islam in the Arabian peninsula. With a formidable and fierce fighting force of ten thousand, they set off to launch an attack on Madinah.

When the holy Prophet Muhammad ﷺ became aware of these developments, he called his Companions for consultation. The situation was critical. How could an assault on one small city by a mighty army be stopped? Especially when there was no shortage of adversaries even within the city. One of the Companions, Salman al-Farisi suggested: "In our land of Persia, when an enemy embarks upon an onslaught of this kind, we would stop its advance by digging a trench around the city. With your command a trench can be dug around

Madinah?" The holy Prophet ﷺ welcomed and approved of this suggestion. On the side of the city where the enemy's attack was most likely, the area for the trench was marked out. Groups of ten men were assigned the task of digging a trench forty yards long, with the trench being five yards wide and five yards deep. All of the Muslims took part in the digging of this trench and nobody was exempt. The beloved of Almighty Allah, the holy Prophet Muhammad ﷺ, with a spade in his hands, stood shoulder to shoulder with his servants and occupied himself in the digging of the trench. Again and again, he dug with his spade and shovelled out the soil such that the hair on his blessed body were covered with dust and his blessed skin could not be seen. With his tongue, the holy Prophet ﷺ was repeatedly saying:

إِنَّ الْعَيْشَ عَيْشُ الْآخِرَةِ . فَاغْفِرِ الْأَنْصَارَ وَالْمُهَاجِرَةَ

"The real life is life of the Hereafter. O my Lord! Forgive the ansar (helpers) and the muhajirun (emigrants)."

On hearing this profound supplication in their favour, the noble Companions were overcome with devotion and spiritual intensity. With joy and passion, they would repeat the call:

نَحْنُ الَّذِينَ بَايَعُوا مُحَمَّدًا . عَلَى الْجِهَادِ مَا بَقِينَا أَبَدًا

"We are the ones who have pledged allegiance to Muhammad! As long as we are alive, we will remain occupied in the struggle to raise the word of truth."

'Amr ibn 'Awf reports: "Me, Salman, Hudhayfah, Nu'man and

six of the *ansar* were digging our share of the forty yard trench when suddenly we came across a hard rock. We used all our strength and tried very hard but could not break the rock. So, Salman then went to the holy Prophet ﷺ and said that our arms had tired and our pickaxes had become blunt, yet it seems that the rock does not want to break at all. Hearing this, the holy Prophet ﷺ himself came to us. He took hold of the pickaxe from Salman's hands, proclaimed *Allahu Akbar* (Allah is the Greatest) and struck the rock. With his strike there was a sudden spark and such light emerged as if someone had suddenly lit a lamp in complete darkness, and one third of that rock split and fell apart. The holy Prophet stated: "Allah is the Greatest. I have been granted the keys to Syria. By Allah! I can at this moment see the red palaces of Syria." Then the holy Prophet ﷺ recited the name of Almighty Allah and gave the rock a second blow. It sparked again with light emanating and a second piece from the rock broke off. The holy Prophet ﷺ stated: "Allah is the Greatest. I have been granted the keys to Persia. By Allah! I can at this moment see the white palace of al-Mada'in (Ctesiphon)." On his third blow, whatever was left shattered into small pieces. The holy Prophet ﷺ stated: "Allah is the Greatest. I have been granted the keys to Yemen. By Allah! I can at this moment see the gates of Sana'a." "

The seriousness of the reality on the ground and the situation that confronted the Muslims was not hidden from anyone. All of Arabia was making a charge and heading towards Madinah, and at the same time the presence of the Jews inside Madinah was also posing a threat. In these volatile circumstances when one's own safety was itself uncertain, to foretell victories over the great empires and super powers of the age could only be proclaimed by a true and genuine Messenger of Almighty

Allah, in front of whose eye of prophethood the events of the future are clearly visible and apparent. Later on, it was during the era of the holy Prophet's rightful Caliph, 'Umar ibn al-Khattab al-Faruq, when these empires and kingdoms were conquered by the Muslims, and in this way the holy Prophet's prophecies were fulfilled.

Three days had elapsed in digging the trench and the noble Companions had not been able to even eat one morsel of food. In order to keep their bodies upright, they had each a stone strapped on their bellies. When the pangs of hunger became unbearable to them, they pointed this out to their generous master, the holy Prophet Muhammad ﷺ. In response, the holy Prophet ﷺ graciously lifted his garment and the Companions witnessed an unexpected and surprising scene. The noble Companions had each strapped a stone to his belly, but this leader of both worlds, the holy Prophet ﷺ, had strapped two stones on his blessed belly. Suddenly all grievances subsided and feelings of despair faded away.

When one of the holy Prophet's Companions, Jabir, witnessed this incident, he could no longer remain patient. He requested leave from the holy Prophet ﷺ and immediately went home. He informed his wife that today he had seen the holy Prophet ﷺ in a state of severe hunger and asked her whether she had anything to eat. She replied that there were a few kilograms of oats and a young goat in the house. Jabir narrates: "She got the pot of oats, crushed the oats and made dough. I slaughtered the goat and placed the meat in a pot on the stove to cook. Soon it was almost sunset. Our routine was that we would dig the trench all day and in the evening everyone would go to their homes. The holy Prophet ﷺ would also return home in the evening. As I was about to leave my house and go back to the trench, my wife asked me not to bring too many people for dinner so that she is not left embarrassed in front of the Prophet ﷺ and his Companions for not preparing enough food. I reassured her, then went to the holy Prophet ﷺ and very quietly and secretly said: "O Allah's Messenger! We have prepared quite a small amount of food. I invite you to please come for dinner and bring one or two people with you." The holy Prophet ﷺ placed his fingers in between mine and asked: "How much have you cooked?" I replied: "A little." The holy Prophet ﷺ responded: "This is a lot and it is very pure. Listen! Do not take the cooking pot off the stove until I arrive and do not make bread." Then the holy Prophet ﷺ in a raised voice said: "O people of the trench! Jabir has cooked dinner for you. Come, let us all go and eat." Allah's Messenger ﷺ walked in front and the people followed from behind. I was sweating in embarrassment and only Allah truly knew what state I was in. I said to myself that the whole of humanity is on its way, this is very embarrassing, only a few oats and small goat!"

Jabir continues: "On arriving home, I said to my wife: "O fortunate one! The holy Prophet Muhammad ﷺ has come with the *ansar* and the *muhajirun* as well as other people." She asked: "Jabir! Was it you or the holy Prophet ﷺ who invited the people?" I told her that the holy Prophet ﷺ invited the people, to which she said: "Then there is no need to worry. Let them all come. Allah and His Messenger know best. Whatever we had, we had indeed informed him of it." With these words of hers, my anxiety began to reduce. Then the holy Prophet ﷺ came inside and instructed to allow ten guests in at a time. I presented the dough to the holy Prophet ﷺ who placed his blessed saliva in it and prayed for blessings. He then instructed that we begin making bread from the dough. Then the holy Prophet ﷺ went to the stove where the cooking put was located and there too he placed his blessed saliva in the pot and prayed for blessings. He then instructed that we begin to serve the food from the pot to the guests whilst keeping the pot covered. We continued to serve the food and we became completely surprised that so many people had dinner, but the dough did not lessen and neither did the meat curry in the pot run out. One thousand people ate dinner at our place that evening. The pot remained full and the dough did not at all reduce. Then the holy Prophet ﷺ said to us: "Now eat yourself and distribute the food as a gift to your relatives and friends, for everyone is experiencing a famine." We began distributing and serving food for quite some time and the holy Prophet ﷺ remained with us during this time. Afterwards, as soon as the holy Prophet ﷺ left our house, everything finished."

In short, due to the continuous efforts of the holy Prophet ﷺ and the noble Companions, the trench was dug and completed within a short period of six days. The holy Prophet ﷺ then stationed three thousand soldiers from the Muslim army in battle formation at appropriate positions. As soon as the Muslims had finalised their preparations, the mighty army of the Arab polytheists arrived within the boundaries of the city of Madinah. The polytheists had planned that they would launch a ferocious attack and flood the small city of Madinah like a tsunami and within a short time they will wipe out the Muslims. But when they discovered a very wide and deep trench in their path, they were shocked and taken aback. They had never contemplated about an obstacle of this kind. Constrained by the presence of this trench, they pitched their tents on the opposite side of the trench, encircled the Muslims and waited for the right time to launch an attack.

One day during this time, a well-known horseman among the Arabs, 'Amr ibn 'Abd Wudd, began to move around the trench with his comrades. He came across a spot where the trench was relatively narrower and so he kicked the horse with his heel and galloped forward. The horse jumped with great speed and landed on the other side of the trench. 'Amr called out and challenged vociferously: "Is there anyone who will fight me in combat?" Hearing this challenge from this unbeliever, the lion of Almighty Allah, 'Ali ibn Abi Talib, came forward waving his sword in the air. The two men began to fight courageously and the cloud of dust around them obscured them from sight. The beloved of Almighty Allah, the holy Prophet ﷺ, prayed for 'Ali's victory with tears in his eyes. When the cloud of dust settled down after a few minutes, everyone saw that the enemy lay dead on the ground and 'Ali stood victorious above him. From the time this incident took place, the army of unbelievers maintained the siege of Madinah for one month, but not one of them could find the courage to move forward.

The Jewish tribe of Banu Qurayzah, which remained settled in Madinah, also broke the peace treaty and decided to attack the Muslims from inside Madinah. The holy Prophet Muhammad ﷺ despatched five hundred soldiers to go and protect the city of Madinah from any internal threat. The soldiers patrolled the streets of Madinah making the call *Allahu Akbar* (Allah is the Greatest); the whole city would echo with this call. The Jews hesitated due to this timely action of the Muslims and realised that the Muslims were not complacent and any ill-advised venture they pursue inside Madinah against the Muslims may lead to themselves suffering its consequences for generations to come.

During this time also, the holy Prophet's aunt, Safiyyah, observed that a man from the conspiring Jewish tribe was suspiciously roaming around the fortress where the Muslim women and children were staying. As the man approached the defensive structure where she was present, Safiyyah picked a log and courageously hit him across his head killing him. Safiyyah dragged the body and left it where the Jews were settled and were plotting their attacks against the Muslims inside Madinah. Seeing the dead body of their comrade, the Jews became more certain that despite being occupied near the trench, the Muslims had also made arrangements to protect their women and children in the city. If any of them tried to harm them, they may face terrible consequences.

During the siege, the polytheists tried again and again to cross over the trench, but they did not succeed. From both sides, the pelting of stones and the launching of arrows continued towards each other. One day, the army of the unbelievers collectively attacked the area where the holy Prophet's tent had been pitched. All of the Muslims gathered near the holy Prophet's tent and the battle with arrows, stones and spears continued throughout the day, such that the Muslims did not have time to perform the noon (*zuhr*), mid-afternoon (*'asr*), sunset (*maghrib*) and nightfall (*'isha'*) prayers.

At night when the holy Prophet Muhammad ﷺ returned to his tent, he instructed Bilal to make the call to prayer (*adhan*). After that, Bilal said the call for initiating the prayer (*iqamah*) and everyone performed the *zuhr* prayer being led by the their master, the holy Prophet ﷺ. Following the *zuhr* prayer, they performed the *'asr, maghrib* and *'isha'* prayers in the same manner with an *iqamah* before each prayer. Although their bodies were tired and exhausted due to fierce fighting throughout the day and half of the night, nevertheless, when they stood in prayer and prostrated before their Generous and Merciful Lord, it was as if their tiredness had vanished and they were completely fresh and full of new energy.

As the unbelievers' siege continued and was prolonged, it gave rise to all kinds of rumours and suspicions. The enemies of Islam began to doubt and mistrust one another. Their provisions also slowly began to diminish and the coming cold weather began to dampen their spirits.

On one night, a severe windstorm struck. Their tents were uprooted, cooking pots overturned, and their horses broke loose and dispersed. A sense of despair and desperation spread throughout the entire army and they feared that the storm would destroy them. Abu Sufyan, who was the mastermind of this onslaught, mounted his camel and said: "I am leaving and you all should leave too." Watching the leader and commander-in-chief display such cowardice and flee, the rest of the Quraysh also found it to be safer if they too fled and went back.

During this long siege of one month, about three or four enemies of Islam were killed and about six or seven Muslims were martyred. In order to take the dead bodies of their comrades, 'Amr ibn 'Abd Wudd and Nawfal, back with them, the unbelievers offered ten thousand *dirhams* (silver coins) in return for each of the bodies. The holy Prophet Muhammad ﷺ

returned their corpses without taking anything in return and said: "We do not make a living by selling the dead."

Banu Qurayzah Campaign

Previously, some of the Jewish tribes had been banished from the city of Madinah on account of their violation of the terms of the treaty and their conspiracies against the holy Prophet Muhammad ﷺ. Remaining in Madinah were the Jews from the tribe of Banu Qurayzah, who according to the treaty should have participated in the city's defence too, but they did a lot worse than simply breaching the constitution.

After the Battle of the Trench (*khandaq*), the Muslims went and surrounded the fortress of Banu Qurayzah, because they had breached the terms of the treaty and had tried to inflict harm upon the Muslims from inside Madinah. The siege of their fortress lasted for twenty-five days, during which arrows were fired and stones pelted at one another. In the end, the Banu Qurayzah Jews came out from their fortress and surrendered.

Both parties agreed to appoint Ṣa'd ibn Mu'adh as arbitrator in making a decision regarding the fate of the people of Banu Qurayzah. After receiving assurances that they would all comply with his judgement, Sa'd announced his decision that men who were old enough to fight were to be executed, and women and children to be taken prisoners. This was because the treachery of the tribe of Banu Qurayzah came at the most critical point when the whole of Arabia had mounted an attack on the small city settlement of Madinah with an army of ten thousand and the Muslims were fighting for their survival in a battle of life and death.

This was an extremely difficult situation. If Almighty Allah had not created such means through His divine power by way of which the enemies of Islam suffered despair in the end and lost their will to continue with their siege or to launch their offensive, then consider yourself that had the unbelievers attacked from the outside and the Banu Qurayzah from the inside, the Muslims would have been annihilated.

Questions:

1. What was the fighting strength of the Muslims and the enemies of Islam in the Battle of the Trench?
2. Who gave the suggestion to dig the trench, and how long did it take to complete?
3. Recount an interesting incident that took place during the days that the trench was being dug.
4. Name the Jewish tribe in Madinah who broke the treaty, and how did the tribe in the end surrender?
5. Narrate in detail the dinner invitation of Jabir.

CHAPTER 27

TREATY OF HUDAYBIYAH

The *ansar* (helpers) and the *muhajirun* (emigrants) in the city of Madinah longed to visit the House of Almighty Allah in Makkah, the Ka'bah. Hence, on the first day of Dhu'l-Qa'dah in the sixth year after the emigration (*hijrah*), the holy Prophet Muhammad ﷺ with fourteen hundred Companions set off heading for Makkah. As the holy Prophet ﷺ had only intended to go and perform the lesser pilgrimage (*'umrah*), therefore, they took with them only animals to sacrifice and did not take any weapons of war. When this caravan reached the place called Dhu'l-Hulayfah, five to six miles outside Madinah, the Muslims entered the state of pilgrim sanctity by changing into their *ihram* (pilgrim dress). When the Quraysh heard the news of the holy Prophet's journey to Makkah, all kinds of fears and apprehensions took root in their hearts. They felt that the intention of pilgrimage by the Muslims was merely an excuse and their real aim was to capture Makkah. They came to the decision that they will not allow the Muslims to set foot in the city of Makkah under any circumstances.

As the Muslims arrived nearer to Makkah, they pitched their camp at a place called Hudaybiyah. The leaders of Makkah sent 'Urwah ibn Mas'ud al-Thaqafi to negotiate with the Muslims and persuade them to return back. 'Urwah held a discussion with the holy Prophet Muhammad ﷺ. He was convinced that the holy Prophet ﷺ neither intended to fight with the people of Makkah nor to even capture Makkah, rather the holy Prophet ﷺ had come with his Companions only wanting to perform *'umrah* of the House of Almighty Allah. Accordingly, 'Urwah informed the leaders of Makkah of his findings and advised them to refrain from confronting the Muslims, since they would return to Madinah after spending a few days in Makkah.

'Urwah ibn Mas'ud also told the people of Makkah that he had visited the royal courts of the Caesar of Rome and the Chosroes of Persia as well as the palaces of other emperors and rulers, but he had never seen anywhere anything like the level of deep devotion and extent of selfless affection that existed in the hearts of the holy Prophet Muhammad's followers for him. 'Urwah said to them: "If he spits, they collect the blessed saliva in the palms of their hands as a blessing. If he performs ablution, they do not let a drop of his water reach the ground, rather they move forward to catch the water and wipe their faces and their chests with it. If he signals them to do something, they rush to supersede each other in fulfilling that task. Therefore, confronting the Muslims is not something that you are capable of." However, the people of Makkah remained stubborn in their intent.

The holy Prophet ﷺ sent 'Uthman al-Ghani to inform the leaders of Makkah of the situation that the Muslims had not come for a battle; they are in the state of pilgrim sanctity dressed as pilgrims, they have brought sacrificial animals with them and have not brought any weapons to fight with. The leaders of Makkah replied that they had sworn not to allow the Muslims to enter the city of Makkah, the Muslims should go back this time and they will think about allowing the Muslims to come for the *'umrah* the following year. They further said to 'Uthman: "We will not allow any other Muslim to enter Makkah nor to circumambulate (*tawaf*) around the Ka'bah, but since you are now our guest, you may continue." To this 'Uthman replied that he would not perform *tawaf* of the Ka'bah until his beloved and Messenger of Almighty Allah had not done so.

As the leaders of Makkah kept 'Uthman occupied in discussion with them in Makkah, meanwhile a rumour spread that 'Uthman had been martyred in Makkah. The holy Prophet ﷺ announced that they would not leave from that place until the blood of 'Uthman had not been avenged. The holy Prophet ﷺ called on the Companions to pledge allegiance that they would struggle and be ready to give their lives for this cause. The noble Companions rushed forward to the holy Prophet ﷺ and began to pledge their allegiance. This oath of allegiance became to be known as the Pledge of Contentment (*bay'at al-ridwan*), for Almighty Allah gave the glad tidings of Him being pleased with those who made this pledge of allegiance.

When the noble Companions had made their pledges, the holy Prophet Muhammad ﷺ placed his right hand on his left hand and supplicated to Almighty Allah: "O Allah! Take this pledge to be from the hand of 'Uthman, since he has gone to fulfil Your command and that of Your Prophet." The holy Prophet ﷺ

made this pledge on behalf of 'Uthman because he knew that the reports about 'Uthman's death were not true. The wisdom in making this pledge was to inspire awe in the hearts of the unbelievers as they hear about the firm resolve of the Muslims and dispel from their hearts any notion of fighting a battle with the Muslims. Consequently, this is exactly what happened. When the people of Makkah heard the news of this pledge, they were stunned by the sheer determination of the Muslims. Their stubbornness soon evaporated and they sent Suhayl ibn 'Amr to negotiate a peace deal with the Muslims.

After lengthy negotiations and a long discussion, when they had agreed on the terms of the peace treaty, 'Ali ibn Abi Talib began writing the agreement with the words: "This is the treaty of peace upon which Muhammad, the Messenger of Allah …" Hearing these words, Suhayl became outraged and said: "This is what the actual dispute is about. If we accepted you as Messenger of Allah, why would we be opposing you? Write the words *Muhammad, the son of 'Abdullah*." So, the holy Prophet ﷺ instructed: "O 'Ali! I am Muhammad, *the son of 'Abdullah*; write these words and wipe out the words *the Messenger of Allah*." 'Ali replied: "O Allah's Messenger! I cannot bear to do this." So the holy Prophet ﷺ said: "Show me where you have written these words." Then the holy Prophet ﷺ himself erased those words from the treaty.

The words of the Treaty of Hudaybiyah read as follows:

"In your name, O Allah! This is the treaty of peace upon which Muhammad ibn 'Abdullah and Suhayl ibn 'Amr have agreed. They have agreed not to fight and allow their arms to rest for ten years. During this time people shall be secure and remain in peace, and

neither party shall attack the other; no theft and secret damage shall be inflicted, but honesty and honour shall prevail between them. Whichever tribe wishes to enter into a treaty or covenant with Muhammad can do so, and whoever wishes to enter into a treaty or covenant with the Quraysh can do so too. If anyone from Makkah comes without the permission of his guardian to Muhammad, he shall be returned; but if on the other hand anyone of Muhammad's people comes to the Quraysh, he shall not be returned. This year, Muhammad with his Companions will withdraw from Makkah and go back. Next year, he may come to Makkah with his Companions for the purpose of performing the 'umrah and remain for three days, yet without their weapons except for a sword, and with the swords remaining in their sheaths."

Following the conclusion of the treaty, the holy Prophet Muhammad ﷺ and the noble Companions changed their *ihram*, put on their normal garments and in this way came out of the state of pilgrim sanctity. The animals they had brought with them were also sacrificed. The holy Prophet ﷺ had his head shaved and his blessed hairs were lodged on a nearby tree. The people would come and take the hair of the holy Prophet ﷺ as a blessing and those who would take a lot would share them amongst others. Umm 'Ammarah also went and brought back quite a lot of the blessed hair. It was her practice that whenever someone would fall ill, she would wash the blessed hair of the holy Prophet ﷺ in water and then give that water to the one who was ill to drink. With the grace of Almighty Allah and the blessing of that water, the sick would be cured.

Some of the terms and conditions of this treaty were not liked by the Muslims. However, soon afterwards, when the positive effects of this agreement started to become more and more apparent, their concerns and misgivings died down. Since, by agreeing to this treaty, the unbelievers of Makkah had in fact accepted the independent status of the Muslim community. The continuous state of heightened confrontation and ongoing war between Makkah and Madinah ended and restrictions on coming and going came to a close. In addition, this new found state of relative peace resulted in the pace of Islam's preaching and propagation accelerating. Numerous tribes started to enter into the folds of Islam.

In this expedition, the number of followers with the holy Prophet Muhammad ﷺ was around fourteen hundred people, but when he set out towards the conquest of Makkah two years later, this number had turned into a great army of ten thousand people. Abu Bakr al-Siddiq would often say: "There is no victory in Islam greater than the victory of Hudaybiyah, but the minds of the people could not grasp the essence of this secret that was between the Chosen One, Muhammad ﷺ, and his Lord Almighty. I saw Suhayl ibn 'Amr on the occasion of the Farewell Pilgrimage that he would be placing the blessed hair of the holy Prophet ﷺ on his own eyes. At that moment, I remembered that objection of Suhayl to the writing of *Muhammad, the Messenger of Allah,* on the day of Hudaybiyah. So, I glorified Almighty Allah who granted him the ability to accept Islam."

The holy Prophet ﷺ stayed in Hudaybiyah for twenty days. There were around fourteen hundred Companions, their rides and the animals for sacrifice with him. The weather was extremely hot and all the water wells in Hudaybiyah had dried up. So, in desperation the noble Companions worryingly came to the holy Prophet ﷺ. The holy Prophet ﷺ had a little amount of water in a small container with him, with which he was performing the ablution. The Companions said: "At this moment, other than this small amount of water which is present before you for ablution, there is no sign of any water anywhere. Great difficulties are arising due to severe thirst." Suddenly, water started to gush out from the fingers of the holy Prophet ﷺ like it gushes out of a fountain. Everyone drank the water and performed ablution. Jabir states: "That day we numbered around fourteen hundred people. Even if we had been one hundred thousand people, the water from the fingers of the holy Prophet ﷺ still would have been enough for all."

The holy Prophet Muhammad ﷺ went and stood on the edge of a dried up well. He asked for some water, washed his mouth with it, supplicated and prayed over it, and then dropped the water into the well. After a short while, the well became full of water. The Muslims drank the water from this well abundantly and gave water to their rides and animals too. This continued and the well remained full of water until the Muslims left that place for good.

PLEDGE OF THE TREE

The Pledge of Contentment (*bay'at al-ridwan*) is also called the Pledge of the Tree (*bay'at al-shajarah*). The tree beneath which the holy Prophet Muhammad ﷺ took the pledge of allegiance form his noble Companions at Hudaybiyah disappeared by the will of Allah due to His divine wisdom. When 'Umar ibn al-Khattab passed by that spot of land some time later, he began searching and tried to find that tree along with some other Companions. When people began to dispute the location of that tree and their differences increased, 'Umar said: "Move on! Move on! The tree has been concealed."

Later on, when 'Umar found out that some people had started to consider some other tree as being the tree of the pledge, he ordered for that particular tree to be cut down.

Questions:

1. What advice did 'Urwah ibn Mas'ud al-Thaqafi give to the people of Makkah?
2. What led to the Pledge of Contentment, and why is it called this?
3. Why did 'Uthman refuse to circumambulate the Ka'bah when he was allowed to do so by the leaders of Makkah?
4. What were the conditions of the Treaty of Hudaybiyah?
5. What was the benefit of this treaty?
6. How did the Companions gain blessings from the hair of the holy Prophet Muhammad ﷺ?
7. In the heat of the desert without water, describe one miracle of the holy Prophet ﷺ regarding water.
8. Why did 'Umar order the alleged tree of the pledge to be cut down?

CHAPTER 28

LETTERS OF INVITATION TO ISLAM

After returning from Hudaybiyah, in the seventh year after the emigration (*hijrah*), the holy Prophet Muhammad ﷺ sent letters to different rulers and emperors in which he invited them, in a simple and appealing manner, to embrace the way of Islam. To authenticate his letters, the holy Prophet ﷺ had a silver ring made, the head of which was also made of silver and was engraved with the words *Muhammad Rasul Allah* (Muhammad, the Messenger of Allah). It was used as a stamp and was the official sacred seal of the holy Prophet ﷺ. Its imprint would appear in the following manner:

Notice that the holy Prophet ﷺ ensured that the divine name *Allah* was engraved at the top, the word *Rasul* (Messenger) in the middle, and his own name *Muhammad* beneath that.

It was also a miracle of the mercy for the world, the holy Prophet Muhammad ﷺ, that the person who was selected to go as an emissary to a certain country, Almighty Allah made the emissary of the holy Prophet ﷺ an expert in the native language of the country he was being sent to, so that he could convey the message clearly and in a forthright manner.

NEGUS, KING OF ABYSSINIA

When Negus (al-Najashi), who was the King of Abyssinia, received the letter of the holy Prophet Muhammad ﷺ, he welcomed it with great respect and reverence and placed it on his eyes. After reading the letter, he said: "I bear witness that you are the untaught (*ummi*) Prophet the People of the Book (*ahl al-kitab*) are waiting for. I have embraced Islam at the hand of your cousin, Ja'far."

Negus passed away in the ninth year after emigration and the holy Prophet ﷺ performed his funeral prayer in Madinah with his Companions.

HERACLIUS, EMPEROR OF BYZANTIUM

The Byzantine Empire (Byzantium) was the eastern half of the Roman Empire. When Heraclius, who was the Emperor of Byzantium, read the letter of the holy Prophet Muhammad ﷺ, he was struck by so much awe and wonder at the prophetic majesty that drops of sweat began to fall from his forehead. He took the holy Prophet's emissary to a secluded place and said: "By God! I know Muhammad ﷺ is a true Prophet of Almighty Allah. All his characteristics and qualities are mentioned in our books. But I fear that if I was to declare my faith in him, the Romans will not spare my life."

Heraclius carefully placed the letter in a cylinder case made of gold and respectfully put it away for safe-keeping. The emperors who came after Heraclius held the letter in high esteem and reverence too, and they always placed it in a respectful and honourable place.

AL-MUQAWQIS, VICEGERENT OF EGYPT

Al-Muqawqis, who was the vicegerent and ruler of Egypt, received the letter of the holy Prophet Muhammad ﷺ with due respect and dignity. He preserved it in a beautiful small ivory chest.

In response, al-Muqawqis wrote a letter in which he said: "I was aware that a Prophet was soon to come, but I thought that he would emerge from the land of Syria. Now, he has come in Arabia and my people will not accept this religion. If I accept Islam, then I will be forced to give up this crown and throne of mine, and that is something I do not want to do."

PARVEZ, CHOSROES II OF PERSIA

On reading the letter of the holy Prophet Muhammad ﷺ, Parvez, who was Chosroes II of Persia, lost control of himself out of sheer anger and resentment. In a disrespectful and degrading manner, he tore the letter into pieces.

When he was informed about the terrible reaction of Parvez, the holy Prophet ﷺ remarked: "He has torn my letter into pieces, Almighty Allah has torn his kingdom into pieces." It was only a few days later that Parvez's son attacked his own father by night stabbing him in his stomach. He then took over the empire himself becoming its ruler, but soon this Sasanian Empire sank into anarchy.

Questions:

1. What were the words of the seal of prophethood, and how were they engraved in the holy Prophet's ring?
2. Recount how Negus embraced Islam?
3. Why did Heraclius of Byzantium and al-Muqawqis of Egypt decline to embrace Islam?
4. What was the consequence of the manner in which Chosroes II of Persia insulted the holy Prophet's letter?

CHAPTER 29

CONQUEST OF KHAYBAR

After arriving in Madinah from Hudaybiyyah, the holy Prophet Muhammad ﷺ became aware that the Jews of Khaybar had joined forces with other polytheist tribes of Arabia and were planning an attack on Madinah. So, in the month of Muharram in the seventh year after the emigration (*hijrah*), the holy Prophet ﷺ taking sixteen hundred Companions with him set off heading for Khaybar. Although the distance between Madinah and Khaybar was around 156 kilometres, nonetheless, the army of Islam completed this journey quickly, arriving at Khaybar within three days. The Jews of Khaybar had built fortresses around their various settlements. When they saw the Muslims entering Khaybar, all of the Jews took up battle positions securing themselves in their fortified citadels.

The holy Prophet ﷺ divided the Muslim soldiers into small battalions and assigned each group to surround the different forts. The aim was to keep the inhabitants of each fort preoccupied in their own defence and prevent them from uniting their fragmented forces to confront the Muslims. The bulk of the Muslim army focused its strength on one fort and would launch an attack. After conquering the fort, the army would then move on to attack the next fort, whilst the other smaller battalions kept the inhabitants of the other forts busy in trying to defend themselves.

The army of Islam first surrounded the fort of Na'im. On that day, the holy Prophet ﷺ was riding a horse, wearing two body armours and a helmet, and held a lance and a shield in his hands. The Jewish archers kept targeting the Muslims firing their arrows at them, and the Muslims kept using the same arrows and launching them back. In spite of several days of intense fighting, this fort was not conquered. Then one day, the holy Prophet ﷺ said: "Tomorrow I will give this flag to the individual by whose efforts, Almighty Allah will grant victory in conquering this fort." All the soldiers heard this statement of the holy Prophet ﷺ. They spent that night in anticipation and suspense. Every one of them wished to be chosen for this privilege. In the morning, they all came to the holy Prophet ﷺ. They were all greatly anxious to know the name of the fortunate person who was about to be given the flag.

After performing the Friday Prayer on that day, the holy Prophet ﷺ asked for the flag, stood up and announced: "Where is 'Ali?" He was informed that 'Ali was resting in his tent due to both of his eyes being infected and in pain. The holy Prophet ﷺ sent for him. Muhammad ibn Muslimah narrates that he went to call 'Ali ibn Abi Talib, and since 'Ali had a bandage on his head covering his eyes, he held his hand and brought him to the holy Prophet ﷺ. The mercy for the world, the holy Prophet Muhammad ﷺ, asked: "O 'Ali! What happened to you?" 'Ali replied that his eyes were hurting and that he could not see anything in front of him. The holy Prophet ﷺ asked 'Ali to come closer to him. 'Ali ibn Abi Talib then states: "I moved closer to the holy Prophet ﷺ. He placed my head in his lap, took his blessed saliva in his hands and wiped his hands over my eyes. I was immediately cured and it was as though I had never had any pain or ailment in my eyes." It was due to the blessing of that blessed saliva that 'Ali ibn Abi Talib never again throughout his life felt any pain or difficulty in his eyes.

Afterwards, the holy Prophet ﷺ gave the flag to 'Ali. 'Ali took hold of the flag and headed for the fort. There he stood in front of the fort and firmly planted his flag in the ground. A combat warrior by the name of Marhab, who was known to have the strength of fighting a thousand men, was sent out from the Jewish side ferociously waving his sword in the air. Singing his battle call, he challenged the Muslims:

قَدْ عَلِمَتْ خَيْبَرُ أَنِّي مَرْحَبُ . شَاكِي السِّلَاحِ بَطَلٌ مُجَرَّبُ

"The whole of Khaybar knows that Marhab I am!
Armed with weapons, brave and practiced I am!"

In reply to this, the lion of Almighty Allah, 'Ali ibn Abi Talib, stepped forward reciting his blessed call:

أَنَا الَّذِي سَمَّتْنِي أُمِّي حَيْدَرًا . كَلَيْثِ غَابَاتٍ كَرِيهِ الْمَنْظَرِ

"The one whose mother named him Haydar I am!
Impressive and formidable as the lions of the jungles I am!"

With his sword named *dhu'l-fiqar* in his hand, 'Ali ibn Abi Talib went into combat with Marhab giving his head a fast and fierce blow. The sword cut right through the metal helmet down to his teeth. With the death of Marhab at the hands of 'Ali in this battle, the Jews of Khaybar lost their courage to fight, and after some small fights and skirmishes and some negotiations, one by one the fortified citadels and forts were gradually conquered. In the Battle of Khaybar, fifteen Muslims were martyred and ninety-three enemy fighters were killed.

Sun Rises Back

After the Conquest of Khaybar, the army of Islam was on its way back to Madinah when one day during this return journey, the holy Prophet Muhammad ﷺ was resting with his head in the lap of 'Ali ibn Abi Talib. The holy Prophet ﷺ was in a deep state of receiving divine revelation. 'Ali had not yet performed the mid-afternoon (*'asr*) prayer and the sun then set. As the sun had set, the holy Prophet ﷺ opened his eyes and asked: "O 'Ali! Have you offered the *'asr* prayer?"

'Ali replied that he had not done so. So, the holy Prophet ﷺ supplicated to Almighty Allah: "O Allah! 'Ali was occupied in Your obedience and that of Your Messenger. Thus, return the sun that has just set so that he can perform the prayer."

Asma' narrates what she witnessed: "I myself saw the sun setting, but then I saw the sun returning back and rising after it had set behind the horizon. 'Ali got up, perform the ablution and performed the *'asr* prayer. After that, the sun set again."

Questions:

1. Why did the Muslims march towards Khaybar?
2. How was the fort of Na'im conquered?
3. Describe the background to the sun returning back after having set?

CHAPTER 30

EXPEDITION OF DHAT AL-RIQA'

A time came when the tribes of Banu Anmar and Banu Sa'd also began making preparations to launch an attack on the Muslims. On receiving the news of this plot and potential threat, the holy Prophet Muhammad ﷺ together with about four to five hundred Companions set off and soon arrived in the area where the tribes were present. The people quickly retreated into the mountains and in this way accepted their defeat. During this particular expedition, the holy Prophet ﷺ remained away from Madinah for fifteen days, and it was in this journey that so many miracles of the holy Prophet ﷺ occurred that this expedition became known as the expedition of strange happenings (*ghazwat al-a'ajib*).

Some of these miracles are presented here, reading of them will increase faith and love for the holy Prophet ﷺ:

1. One day the holy Prophet ﷺ and the Muslim soldiers dismounted their riding animals for an afternoon siesta

(*qaylula*). Wherever anyone found a good shade, he lay down in it and went to sleep for a while. The holy Prophet ﷺ also rested in the shade of a tree and hung his sword on a branch of the tree. Very quickly everyone fell into deep sleep. Suddenly the voice of the holy Prophet ﷺ rose. The noble Companions got up, immediately rushed to the holy Prophet ﷺ and found a Bedouin sitting next to him. The holy Prophet ﷺ said: "I was asleep. This Bedouin came and unsheathed my sword. I woke up to find him waving my unsheathed sword in his hand. He said: "Tell me who will save you from my sword?" I told him that my Allah will save me."

The Bedouin had become so nervous and struck with awe by the answer of the holy Prophet ﷺ that the sword fell through his hands. The mercy for the world, the holy Prophet Muhammad ﷺ, picked the sword up and said: "Now you tell me who will save you from my blow?" The Bedouin pleaded for mercy and forgiveness.

The holy Prophet ﷺ had pardoned him and let him go. When he got back to his people, he could not resist saying to them: "Today I have come from a person who is the best among all people."

2. Jabir narrates that on the way back from the Expedition of Dhat al-Riqa', they saw a camel fast approaching them and whining. The holy Prophet Muhammad ﷺ asked the Companions whether they knew what the camel had just said to him. The holy Prophet ﷺ then told them that the camel had asked him to intercede and help plead with the owner of the camel. The camel had said: "I have

ploughed his land for many years and now he wants to slaughter me." The holy Prophet ﷺ instructed Jabir to go and call the camel's owner, but Jabir replied by saying that he did not know who the owner was and so could not recognise him. The holy Prophet ﷺ said: "The camel will guide you."

Jabir continues to narrate that the camel walked in front of him and took him to the place where the owner was sitting. Jabir brought the camel's owner to the holy Prophet ﷺ. The mercy for all creatures, the holy Prophet Muhammad ﷺ, then talked to the owner on behalf of the camel convincing him not to slaughter.

3. Imam Muslim has narrated the following incident from Jabir. Jabir says: "We were travelling with Allah's Messenger ﷺ during the Expedition of Dhat al-Riqa' when we came across a green valley. The holy Prophet ﷺ left us to attend to the call of nature. I filled the water container and walked behind him. After going quite far, the holy Prophet ﷺ looked around and still could not locate a secluded place where there was something behind which he could conceal and relieve himself. There were two trees on the edge of the valley. The holy Prophet ﷺ went near one of the trees, held its branch and said: "O tree! Obey me with the command of Allah." The tree immediately began to walk behind him like an obedient camel. When the holy Prophet ﷺ reached the other tree, he held its branch and gave it the same instruction. Consequently, that tree also began to walk behind him like an obedient camel. When the holy Prophet ﷺ reached a location bringing both trees

together, he pulled the two branches of the trees closer to each other and they joined together. The holy Prophet ﷺ then attended to the call of nature behind the trees completely veiled from any view. Afterwards, when the holy Prophet ﷺ came towards me, the two trees separated from each other and returned back to their original places. When the holy Prophet ﷺ reached me, he said: "O Jabir! Have you seen my status?" I replied: "Yes! O Allah's Messenger." "

4. A similar incident has also been narrated by Bazzaz that a Bedouin demanded that the holy Prophet ﷺ shows him some kind of sign which would prove to him that he was indeed the Messenger of Almighty Allah. The holy Prophet ﷺ said to him: "That tree you can see in front of you. Go there and tell the tree that Allah's Messenger is calling you." The Bedouin went to the tree and gave it the message of the holy Prophet ﷺ. The tree immediately swayed to the left and then to the right, pulled its roots up and by, piercing the ground before it, came and stood in front of the holy Prophet ﷺ. Then it said: "Peace be upon you, O Allah's Messenger!" Upon seeing this, the Bedouin became certain of the holy Prophet's prophethood and said: "Now tell the tree to return to its original place." Thus, the tree returned to its original location and dug its roots back into the ground.

   After witnessing this miracle, the Bedouin said: "O Allah's Messenger! Grant me permission to prostrate before you." The holy Prophet Muhammad ﷺ replied: "If I were to give the order of prostration before anyone other than Almighty Allah, I would have ordered the wife to prostrate before her husband." The Bedouin responded: "O Allah's Messenger! If you do not allow me to prostrate before you then permit me to kiss both of your blessed hands and blessed feet." The holy Prophet ﷺ allowed him to kiss his hands and his feet.

In *Qasidat al-Burdah,* Imam Sharaf al-Din al-Busiri has so well stated:

جَاءَتْ لِدَعْوَتِهِ الْأَشْجَارُ سَاجِدَةً . تَمْشِى إِلَيْهِ عَلٰى سَاقٍ بِلَاقَدَمِ

"Upon the holy Prophet's calling, the trees came prostrating; Walking towards him on their trunks without feet."

5. One day, the holy Prophet ﷺ said: "O Jabir! Tell the people to make ablution." But no one had even a drop of water with them. Jabir states that the holy Prophet ﷺ then said to him to go to a particular Companion from the *ansar* (helpers) who may have some water in his water sack. Thus, he found a few drops of water and brought the water to the holy Prophet ﷺ. Then the holy Prophet Muhammad ﷺ instructed him to bring a larger bowl, which Jabir brought forward and placed it in front of him.

The holy Prophet ﷺ stretched his blessed hand in the bowl and asked Jabir to pour a few drops of water over his hand and recite the name of Almighty Allah (*bismillah*) at the same time. Jabir states: "I suddenly saw that fountains of water began to gush out of the holy Prophet's finger, such that all people in the caravan drank the water to their full. When everybody had drank as much as they could and quenched their thirst, the holy Prophet ﷺ lifted his hand out of the bowl. The bowl was still full of water to the top."

Performing the Missed 'Umrah

In the previous year which was the sixth year after emigration (*hijrah*), in the month of Dhu'l-Qa'dah, the holy Prophet Muhammad ﷺ had travelled to Makkah along with around fourteen hundred of his noble Companions with the intention of performing the lesser pilgrimage (*'umrah*). However, the people of Makkah did not allow this and eventually the Treaty of Hudaybiyyah was formulated.

Therefore, one year later again in the month of Dhu'l-Qa'dah, the holy Prophet ﷺ made preparations to travel to Makkah and fulfil the performance of the previously missed *'umrah*. The Companions who went the previous year were given the instruction to get ready. Many other people too began making preparations in order to perform the *'umrah* in the company of the holy Prophet Muhammad ﷺ. As such, the total number of people reached two thousand. With the holy Prophet ﷺ, the Companions too changed their clothes into the sheets of the *ihram* next to the holy Prophet's Mosque and entered into the state of pilgrim sanctity. They began to recite the *talbiyyah* (pilgrim recital) loudly.

On the morning of the fourth of Dhu'l-Hijjah, this enlightened caravan reached the sanctuary of Makkah. The leaders of the Quraysh left Makkah and climbed up the mountains, so that their eyes do not see the holy Prophet ﷺ. They could not bear to see the illumined face of the holy Prophet ﷺ because of their intense jealousy, enmity and hatred.

Due to the recent fever caught in Yathrib, the Muslims felt physically weak. But the holy Prophet Muhammad ﷺ commanded the noble Companions to complete the first three circuits of the circumambulation (*tawaf*) around the Ka'bah in the state of *raml,* i.e. with shoulders lifted, chest widened and walking briskly, so that the enemy begins to feel their awe and fear them. After witnessing the manner of their *tawaf* with these physical movements and body language, the unbelievers of Makkah were cleared of their misunderstanding that the climate and atmosphere in Yathrib had physically weakened the Muslims. In accordance with their agreement made a year ago, the Muslims stayed in Makkah for three days and on the fourth day left Makkah and departed for Madinah.

Questions:

1. Why did the holy Prophet ﷺ go to Dhat al-Riqa', and how many Companions went with him?
2. How many days was the holy Prophet ﷺ away from Madinah, and what other name is given to this journey?
3. Describe two miracles that occurred during this journey.
4. How did the holy Prophet ﷺ instruct his Companions to perform *tawaf* of the Ka'bah?

CHAPTER 31

BATTLE OF MU'TAH

When the inspiring and astounding message of Islam began to spread outside the boundaries of the Arabian peninsula, the Byzantine Empire (eastern half of the Roman Empire) began to organise a fierce and large enough army to annihilate Islam. In the land of Syria, the appointed ruler had already decreed that any Syrian citizen who accepts Islam will be executed.

Furthermore, one of the rulers appointed by the Emperor had murdered Harith ibn 'Umayr, who was an emissary sent as an envoy by the holy Prophet Muhammad ﷺ, at a place called Mu'tah. It was not permitted to kill emissaries of any country or people in the international law that was followed by the empires of that time. Without any provocation, he had killed an ambassador, and this was an unforgivable criminal act. As a result of this deliberate violation of international law which guaranteed immunity for emissaries and envoys, the holy Prophet ﷺ organised a force of three thousand soldiers to avenge for the murder of his martyred Companion.

The holy Prophet ﷺ said: "Zayd ibn Harithah will command this army. If he is martyred, then Ja'far ibn Abi Talib will become its commander-in-chief. If he is martyred too, then 'Abdullah ibn Rawahah will lead the force. If he is also killed in the way of truth, then whoever the Muslims select will become their leader."

The holy Prophet ﷺ handed over the flag of Islam with his blessed hands to Zayd and then instructed the soldiers to first visit the grave of the martyred Harith when they reach that land, then they were to invite all the people there to accept the way of Islam. If they accept the invitation then that would be better, otherwise seeking help from Almighty Allah, they were to fight them for breaching the code of international relations by murdering an envoy whose protection was guaranteed. If the matter did eventually come to battle, then the holy Prophet Muhammad ﷺ gave the following instructions regarding the etiquettes of war: "In the name of Allah, fight with those who have rejected Him. In doing so, do not betray, deceive and defraud anyone; do not kill a child or a woman; do not assault an elderly person or anyone seeking sanctuary in a place of worship; do not damage a tree nor destroy any house."

The Byzantine Emperor had amassed together a formidable and fearsome force of two hundred thousand soldiers, whereas the number of soldiers in the Muslim army was only three thousand. When the Muslims heard of this, the noble Companions began to consult with one another. Since the holy Prophet ﷺ was not himself present in this expedition to Mu'tah, the noble Companions decided to send a message and inform the holy Prophet ﷺ of this development and then to wait for his command. But the inspiring speech of 'Abdullah ibn Rawahah made everyone re-assess and change the way they were thinking. He stated: "O people! The martyrdom that frightens you is the very one you left your homes to seek. We do not fight with the enemy on the basis of number, strength and quantity. We fight only on the strength of the religion with which Almighty Allah has honoured us. O servants of Allah! Carry on and let us go. You will attain one of the two virtues: victory or martyrdom."

After this inspirational and moving speech, all the Muslim soldiers assumed their battle positions ready to face the mighty Byzantine force. The two armies attacked and began to fight each other. Zayd ibn Harithah courageously attained martyrdom. After him, Ja'far ibn Abi Talib raised the flag of Islam. One of the unbelievers struck and his right hand was chopped, but he immediately picked the flag up with his left hand. The enemy struck again and disjointed his left hand too by a blow with his sword. Ja'far then held on to the flag tightly by pressing it against his chest with his two amputated arms. Due to the loss of blood, he became extremely weak when suddenly the enemy struck with his sword giving a heavy blow that his body split into two. Ja'far attained martyrdom.

After Ja'far, 'Abdullah ibn Rawahah came forward and took hold of the flag. He too fought bravely and then gave his beloved life for the cause of Islam attaining martyrdom. Eventually, these three brave martyrs and devoted followers of the holy Prophet ﷺ were buried in the same grave. May countless blessings and mercies of Almighty Allah be upon the grave where these courageous lions of Islam are resting. *Amin.* When each one of these three commanders-in-chief named by the holy Prophet Muhammad ﷺ had sacrificed their lives in the way of truth, the Muslim soldiers appointed Khalid ibn al-Walid to take the flag of Islam and lead them. Trusting in Almighty Allah, Khalid raised the flag of Islam in his hand. On that day, nine swords one after the other broke in his hands during the intense fighting. In addition, Khalid altered the battle formations and changed the strategy of the Muslims in this battle. The change was so effective that the Byzantine forces assumed that the Muslims had suddenly acquired more ammunition and reinforcements had arrived. Consequently, they lost their footing and their resolve to continue fighting weakened, so they began to retreat. Many of the enemy soldiers were killed and the Muslims acquired a lot of the spoils of war. Astonishingly, only twelve Muslims were martyred in this battle and all the rest of the soldiers returned back to Madinah safe and well.

This fierce battle between Islam and unbelief was taking place in a land very far away from Madinah and the small army of Islam, being led by Khalid ibn al-Walid, was courageously confronting and defeating the enemy. Here in Madinah, the holy Prophet Muhammad ﷺ called the people to *Masjid Nabawi* (Prophet's Mosque) for an important sermon. To listen to the words of their beloved master, the people of Madinah began to rush towards the holy Prophet's Mosque. Within minutes, the entire mosque was filled. The holy Prophet ﷺ stood on the pulpit and, with tears falling from his blessed eyes, he stated: "O people! Almighty Allah has opened up the battleground for me to see and I can observe what is happening in the battle. The first flagbearer of the army of Islam, Zayd attained martyrdom. Then Ja'far and after him 'Abdullah ibn Rawahah have been martyred. Eventually, a sword from the swords of Allah, Khalid ibn al-Walid, raised the flag of Islam, such that under his leadership the Muslims achieved victory."

One day, the holy Prophet ﷺ was sitting in the company of his noble Companions. The holy Prophet ﷺ raised his head towards the sky and said: "And peace be upon you too, and the mercy of Allah." Those who were present questioned as to whose greeting the holy Prophet ﷺ had just responded. The holy Prophet ﷺ said: "Just now Ja'far ibn Abi Talib went passed me with a group of angels. He greeted me and I returned the greeting." On another occasion, the holy Prophet Muhammad ﷺ said: "Last night I went to Paradise. There I saw that Ja'far ibn Abi Talib was flying with the angels. Due to him having his two arms cut in battle, Almighty Allah granted him two wings."

With this battle, the Muslim army for the first time confronted one of the greatest empires of the day, the Byzantine army. The Muslims returned to Madinah without great losses despite facing an organised army much more superior in terms of numbers and strength.

Questions:

1. What was the relative strength of the Muslim army and that of the Byzantine army in the Battle of Mu'tah?
2. What was the motivational speech of 'Abdullah ibn Rawahah, and what was its background?
3. During the battle taking place in Mu'tah, what did the

holy Prophet ﷺ say in his Mosque in Madinah?

4. What instructions did the holy Prophet ﷺ give to the Muslim soldiers regarding the rules of war?

CHAPTER 32

CONQUEST OF MAKKAH

According to the terms of the Treaty of Hudaybiyah, Arab tribes were free to enter into any agreements and covenants they wished. The tribe of Banu Kinanah entered into an agreement of friendship with the Quraysh and the tribe of Banu Khuza'ah entered into an agreement of friendship with the holy Prophet Muhammad ﷺ. However, the Quraysh in collaboration with Banu Kinanah breached the terms of the Treaty of Hudaybiyah and attacked Banu Khuza'ah, the ally of the Muslims, in the dark hours of the night. To save their lives, the people of Banu Khuza'ah entered the boundaries of the sanctuary of *Haram* in Makkah, but the attackers did not care and violated the sanctity of the *Haram*. They mercilessly killed the people.

A delegation from the tribe of Banu Khuza'ah came to the holy Prophet ﷺ and informed him of the betrayal of the Quraysh to the terms of the treaty and their brutal killings and atrocities committed against their tribe. The holy Prophet ﷺ sent one of his Companions, Damrah, to the people of Makkah in order to put the following three suggestions in front of them:

1. They pay the compensation of blood money for the murdered victims of the tribe of Banu Khuza'ah.
2. They end their agreement of friendship with the tribe of Banu Bakr.
3. They publically and formally declare the end of the Treaty of Hudaybiyyah.

Damrah arrived in Makkah and presented these three suggestions to the Quraysh. The Quraysh responded: "We will not at all accept the first two suggestions. But as for the third suggestion, we accept it and openly announce that the Treaty of Hudaybiyah has been terminated and no longer stands."

On hearing of this situation, the holy Prophet ﷺ set off from Madinah on the 10th of Ramadan, in the eighth year after the emigration (*hijrah*), with a large force of ten thousand people. Arriving close to Makkah, the Muslims set up their camps for the night at a place called Marr al-Zahran. Each person was instructed to light a small fire in front of his tent, as such the entire valley began to illuminate and glow with ten thousand flares.

When Abu Sufyan and Hakim ibn Hizam passed by this valley, they became increasingly worried and nervous seeing so many tents. The Muslims caught up with them and brought them to the holy Prophet Muhammad ﷺ. The holy Prophet ﷺ invited them to accept Islam. Although they were not fully inclined towards Islam, nevertheless, the situation on the ground and the prevailing circumstances compelled them to embrace Islam. After accepting Islam, Abu Sufyan requested safety for the inhabitants of Makkah. The holy Prophet Muhammad ﷺ said: "Whoever enters the house of Abu Sufyan is safe; whoever enters the house of Hakim ibn Hizam is safe; whoever enters the mosque is safe; and whoever closes the door of his house is also safe."

Abu Sufyan returned to Makkah ahead of the army of Islam and announced to everyone: "O people of Makkah! Embrace Islam and you will be saved. The holy Prophet ﷺ has come. He has such a formidable army that you will not be able to confront it." Abu Sufyan further announced the guarantee of safety saying: "Go inside your homes and close your doors; no one will harm you."

Meanwhile, the holy Prophet ﷺ divided the ten thousand strong Muslim army into units and appointed a commander for each unit. He then instructed them to enter Makkah from different directions emphasising that they must keep their swords sheathed. They were not to unsheathe their swords, unless the unbelievers attacked them first. Thus, apart from Khalid ibn al-Walid, no one else experienced any resistance and no one dared to attack them as they entered Makkah. However, an armed group from amongst the Quraysh attacked from one direction, where Khalid was entering the city from. In response, he allowed his group of soldiers to retaliate. In this quarrel, fifteen men from the unbelievers lost their lives and only two Muslims were martyred.

It was the day of Monday, the 20th of Ramadan. The holy Prophet Muhammad ﷺ accompanied by ten thousand of his Companions comes very close to the House of Almighty Allah, the Ka'bah, and raises the call *Allahu Akbar* (Allah is the Greatest). In response, the devoted Muslims also raised the call *Allahu Akbar* with such passion and zeal that the walls and buildings, streets and markets, in the city of Makkah all trembled and echoed with this profound call. The leader of all Prophets, the holy Prophet Muhammad ﷺ, riding his camel began to go around and circumambulate around the Ka'bah. At that time, there were three hundred and sixty idols placed in and around the Ka'bah.

The true guide, the holy Prophet Muhammad ﷺ, was pointing his staff at these idols and one by one whichever idol he pointed towards, it immediately fell on its face. There was a large idol, Hubal, erected near the door of the Ka'bah. Coming around the Ka'bah, when the holy Prophet ﷺ came near this largest idol, he instructed that it be destroyed. At that moment, Zubayr said to Abu Sufyan: "O Abu Sufyan! Just look at the fate of your false god. On the day of Uhud, you were proud of its help and were shouting in its praise." Abu Sufyan responded: "Leave those things aside today. I have witnessed that if there was any other deity other than the God of Muhammad ﷺ, then the situation would not have been the way it is today."

After completing the circumambulation (*tawaf*) of the Ka'bah, when the holy Prophet ﷺ dismounted from his camel, there were so many people present that there was no space at all to stand in the courtyard. People spread out the palms of their hands and, by placing the feet of the holy Prophet ﷺ on their hands, the holy Prophet ﷺ came off the camel and lowered to the ground. The holy Prophet ﷺ proceeded first to the Station of Ibrahim (*maqam Ibrahim*) and performed two units of prayer for completing *tawaf* of the Ka'bah. He then went to the well of Zamzam, drank the blessed water and performed ablution with it. During ablution, whatever drops of water trickled down the holy Prophet's pure skin, the noble Companions would eagerly move forward, collect it in the palms of their hands and wipe it over their faces and chests. By now, the unbelievers of Makkah had also gathered around and were too standing in the courtyard of the Ka'bah. On witnessing this display of reverence, profound affection and devoted acts of love, the unbelievers of Makkah spoke out: "No king of the world has ever attained such a status. Never have we seen or heard of such a spectacle." After this, the holy Prophet ﷺ entered the Ka'bah and went inside, where he performed the prayer of gratitude.

General Amnesty

Upon completing his prayer and prostrating before Almighty Allah in gratitude inside the Ka'bah, the holy Prophet ﷺ came out. In this multitude of people, he addressed the audience and asked: "O people of Quraysh! How do you think I am about to treat you?" In a humble manner, they all replied: "We are hopeful of only good from our noble brother."

The holy Prophet Muhammad ﷺ then stated: "May Almighty Allah forgive your sins. Today, I do not hold you to account. So, go! From me you are free!"

What a display of mercy! Keeping the history of mankind clearly in view and taking the past condition of humanity into consideration, let us review and again deeply reflect on this display of forgiveness and pardon. Who were the people the holy Prophet Muhammad ﷺ was addressing? Who were the people he had unprecedentedly forgiven and pardoned beyond compare, at a time when he had all means and power in worldly terms to do as he wished with them? Surely they were:

1. Those unfortunate people who accused and labelled the holy Prophet ﷺ as being a magician, madman and liar.
2. Those stone-hearted people who besieged and kept the holy Prophet ﷺ in exile for three years in the Valley of Abu Talib.
3. Those who conspired to murder the holy Prophet ﷺ, compelled him to leave his home of Makkah and go into exile in a far-away land.
4. Those who usurped and took hold of the wealth and properties of the Muslims who were forced to emigrate from Makkah.
5. Those brutal people who martyred the holy Prophet's uncle, Hamzah, and then mutilated his ears and nose, and sliced open his chest taking out his liver.
6. Those who attacked the small city of Madinah with an army of ten thousand soldiers with the aim of wiping out the Muslims.
7. Those who stopped the holy Prophet ﷺ outside Makkah at Hudaybiyah, did not allow him to enter the city of Makkah to perform the *'umrah* and had a peace treaty agreed with him based on their own terms and unfair conditions.
8. Those who mercilessly attacked the tribe of Banu Khuza'ah who had entered into an agreement and allied with the holy Prophet ﷺ, and then disregarded the sanctity of the *Haram* and continued their murder.

There exists no other example in the history of mankind that can compare to the standard and exemplar of forgiveness and pardon demonstrated by the mercy for the world, the holy Prophet Muhammad ﷺ, at the conquest of Makkah. Seeing such generosity, nobleness and magnanimity of the holy Prophet ﷺ, the people of Makkah began to flock forward in large groups and embraced Islam by pledging their allegiance at the hands of the holy Prophet Muhammad ﷺ.

KEY TO THE KA'BAH

Before emigrating from Makkah, one day the holy Prophet Muhammad ﷺ asked the keyholder of the Ka'bah, 'Uthman ibn Talhah, for permission to enter the Ka'bah, but he refused in a very rude manner. The holy Prophet ﷺ politely responded to him: "O 'Uthman! Remember that a day is going to come when you will see this key to be in my hand, and I will give it to whoever I wish." Hearing this, 'Uthman became agitated and said: "Will the honour and dignity of the Quraysh be reduced to dust on that day? Only then can such a revolution take place." The holy Prophet ﷺ replied: "O 'Uthman! The day this key will be in my hand, the Quraysh will not be dishonoured and disgraced on that day, rather their honour and prestige on that day will be high and shining bright like the midday sun." 'Uthman himself says that those words of the holy Prophet ﷺ were so powerful that they became imprinted in his heart and mind.

On the day the conquest of Makkah took place, 'Uthman ibn Talhah handed the key to the Ka'bah over to the holy Prophet ﷺ on his command. The holy Prophet ﷺ then said: "O 'Uthman! Do you remember that day when I told you that a day is going to come when you will see this key to be in my hand, and I will give it to whoever I wish." 'Uthman replied: "O Allah's Messenger! Indeed that is exactly what you said, and I bear witness that you are the Messenger of Allah."

The leader of both worlds, the holy Prophet Muhammad ﷺ, gave the key back to 'Uthman and said: "O 'Uthman! I am not only giving you this key, but I am granting it to your future generations too until the Day of Judgement. Whoever takes this key that I have granted away from you, he will be the one who is unjust and a wrongdoer." Today, even after fourteen hundred years, the key to the Ka'bah remains in the possession of 'Uthman's descendants.

Fudalah Accepts Islam

After the conquest of Makkah, Fudalah ibn 'Umayr came to the *Haram*. He saw that the holy Prophet Muhammad ﷺ was performing *tawaf* of the Ka'bah. He thought to himself that on passing by the holy Prophet ﷺ he would attack him with a dagger and put an end to his life.

When he came near, the holy Prophet ﷺ asked: "Are you Fudalah?" He replied that yes he was. The holy Prophet ﷺ then asked: "What were your thinking?" He replied that he was not thinking about anything and was reciting the name of God. Hearing this excuse, the holy Prophet ﷺ smiled and said: "O Fudalah! Seek forgiveness from Almighty Allah." The holy Prophet Muhammad ﷺ then placed his blessed hand over the chest of Fudalah. Fudalah himself then says: "By God! As the holy Prophet ﷺ placed his hand on my chest and lifted it, my heart immediately changed and the holy Prophet ﷺ became the most beloved person to me in the whole world." Fudalah then accepted Islam immediately without hesitation.

Fudalah continues: "When I left the *Haram* and was on my way back home, I passed by the woman with whom I used to sit and pleasurably chat. When I quietly walked passed her this time, she called out: "O Fudalah! Come and let's chat." I replied to her: "I have become a Muslim, and my religion does not allow this." "

WORRY OF THE ANSAR

When the conquest of Makkah had taken place and the glorious flag of Islam began to wave in the blessed atmosphere of Makkah, the *ansar* (helpers) from Madinah began to worry and became concerned and disheartened. They felt very uneasy by the thought that what if their beloved Messenger ﷺ now leaves them and settles down and resides back in his own homeland of Makkah?

Then one day, the holy Prophet Muhammad ﷺ stood on Mount Safa and addressed the *ansar* saying: "Almighty Allah helped me through you, when the people of Makkah abandoned me. This resounding conquest is a result of your sincere efforts. I cannot even think of leaving you and living here. My life and my death will be with you."

After listening to these words of the holy Prophet ﷺ, the anxious hearts of the *ansar* became content and at peace. The leader of both worlds, the holy Prophet ﷺ, further convinced everyone of this decision by promptly acting upon it. After the conquest of Makkah, the holy Prophet ﷺ spent fifteen days in

Makkah. During this time, he made suitable arrangements to manage and administer the affairs and activities of the blessed city of Makkah. It was also within this time that nearly all of the residents of Makkah became Muslims and came into the folds of Islam.

Questions:

1. What led to the holy Prophet ﷺ embarking on a journey to Makkah concerning the tribe of Banu Khuza'ah?
2. What guarantees did the holy Prophet ﷺ give in his conversation with Abu Sufyan at Marr al-Zahran, and how did the Muslims show their strength during the night?
3. What date did the conquest of Makkah take place, and what was the strength of the Muslim army with the holy Prophet ﷺ?
4. Describe the actions of the holy Prophet ﷺ upon entering the *Haram* courtyard, and how did the general amnesty of the holy Prophet ﷺ take place?
5. What was the fate of the keyholder to the Ka'bah?
6. How did Fudalah come to accepting Islam?
7. What thought made the *ansar* uneasy after the conquest of Makkah, and how did the holy Prophet ﷺ remove their feelings of uneasiness?

CHAPTER 33

BATTLE OF HUNAYN

After the conquest of Makkah, majority of the tribes in the Arabian peninsula began to embrace Islam. However, the tribe of Hawazin who lived in the valley of Hunayn, which was near Makkah, immediately started making preparations for an attack on the Muslims. The people from the tribe of Hawazin were successful in encouraging their allies from other tribes to join them, and so with a mighty army of thirty thousand soldiers they were ready to go and confront the Muslims.

There were ten thousand Companions with the holy Prophet Muhammad ﷺ who had come with him from Madinah to Makkah and another two to three thousand new Muslims joined them. The holy Prophet ﷺ asked to borrow arms and other items needed for battle from the people of Makkah and also asked for capital loans from them to fund this expedition.

On the 10th of Shawwal in the eighth year after the emigration (*hijrah*), the holy Prophet ﷺ with his Companions entered the valley of Hunayn. On that day, he was riding his white mule named Duldul, and he was wearing armour over his body and a metal helmet.

The terrain of Hunayn was cluttered with hillocks and a fair amount of small mountains, which were further consisting of deep valleys, narrow passes and safe military outposts. The unbelievers had stationed their experienced archers in these outposts in order to shower down arrows on the Muslim army as it came under their line of attack, and in this way cause the Muslim army to separate and disperse into the surroundings in order to protect themselves.

Consequently, when the first battalion of the Muslim army, which comprised mainly of the new Muslims, crossed these mountainous passes and valleys, the enemy archers hiding in their outposts showered them with their arrows such that the new Muslims lost their balance and footing. Seeing this, the rest of the army too found it difficult to regroup and find a firm footing. Even in these fragile circumstances, the true Prophet of Almighty Allah stood firm as a mountain in steadfastness and called out:

أَنَا النَّبِيُّ لَا كَذِبْ . أَنَا ابْنُ عَبْدِ الْمُطَّلِبْ

"I am the true Prophet; in this there is no lie!
I am the descendant of 'Abd al-Muttalib!"

In a loud voice, the holy Prophet ﷺ called out to the *ansar* (helpers). Very quickly, all of the dispersed *ansar* and the *muhajirun* (emigrants) gathered around the holy Prophet

Muhammad ﷺ waving their swords in the air. They regrouped and stood formidably. Then they marched forward together in an impenetrable tactical formation such that they mounted a vigorous counter offensive which led to the enemy being forced to retreat and flee from their positions. The display of incomparable courage and unique steadfastness by the holy Prophet ﷺ changed the face of battle and led to the enemy's certain victory being turned into a humiliating defeat.

When the polytheists started to flee after experiencing this defeat, the Muslim army charged after them in pursuit. Some of the enemy soldiers were killed and some were taken as prisoners of war. Later on, when a person from the tribe of Hawazin had embraced Islam, he recounted to the Muslims how awe-inspired and overcome by fright they all were on that battle day: "On that day, it felt to us as if every tree and every rock was like a horseman chasing after us. We saw men with fair complexion mounted on piebald horses. Seeing them, we trembled in fear. By God! It felt to us as if we were not fighting anyone from this earth, but were facing those who resided in the heavens." On that day, Almighty Allah sent down five thousand angels in aid of the Muslim soldiers and instilled in the hearts of the Muslims the light of contentment and tranquillity, so that they could fight the enemy in a steadfast manner.

Shaybah Accepts Islam

There were some who joined in this battle with ulterior motives. They entered into the Muslim army in order to seek an opportune moment during the chaos of the fighting when the holy Prophet Muhammad ﷺ would be on his own. They would then be able to kill the holy Prophet ﷺ and satisfyingly cool the fire of revenge that was burning inside them. Shaybah ibn 'Uthman was one of these people.

Shaybah tells his own story: "After the conquest of Makkah when the holy Prophet ﷺ decided to march towards the tribe of Hawazin, I decided to join the Muslim army too. I wanted to find an opportunity when the holy Prophet ﷺ would be on his own and unaware, then I would have attacked him and taken revenge for the death of my father and my uncle. Thus, during that battle when the holy Prophet ﷺ dismounted his mule and disorder ensued in the ranks of the Companions as they dispersed, I unsheathed my sword and decided to strike at the holy Prophet ﷺ from behind him. Suddenly, flames of fire began to rise as an obstacle between me and the holy Prophet ﷺ. My eyes were dazzled by the intense brightness of the flames, and so I moved back. The holy Prophet ﷺ looked back at me and said: "O Shaybah! Why are you going away? Come near me." I went close to the holy Prophet ﷺ. He placed his merciful hand on my chest and supplicated: "O Allah! Cast the devil away from him." Then when I gazed at the holy Prophet Muhammad ﷺ immediately after that, I felt that he was more beloved to me than my own heart, and I thrust myself upon the enemy to defend the holy Prophet ﷺ."

Shaybah continues: "Soon after when the Hawazin had been defeated, the holy Prophet ﷺ looked towards me and said: "All praise is for Almighty Allah who had willed good for you and bestowed His favour upon you. Though you had decided to sink your own boat before." Then the holy Prophet ﷺ told me everything that was in my heart at that time concerning the holy Prophet ﷺ."

SIEGE OF TA'IF

When the unbelievers fled after experiencing defeat in the Battle of Hunayn, a large number of them found refuge in the fortresses of Ta'if. There they began making preparations and amassing their military force together in order to launch another offensive against the Muslims. Ta'if was a very well-fortified town and its people therefore could mount a strong defence. When the holy Prophet Muhammad ﷺ became aware of these military preparations being made against the Muslims in Ta'if, he set off heading for Ta'if accompanied by the Muslim soldiers on the 8th of Shawwal.

The inhabitants of Ta'if were inside the garrisoned fortresses. Arrows were exchanged between the Muslim army and the enemy in their fortresses, as a result of which twelve Muslim soldiers were martyred and many were injured.

The siege of Ta'if was being prolonged, and the crescent for the month of Dhu'l-Qa'dah was soon to appear, during which the Muslims were not permitted to fight in battle. Consequently, the holy Prophet ﷺ lifted the siege and announced to return back. However, not long after, the people of Ta'if announced their obedience to the holy Prophet Muhammad ﷺ; they came to the city of Madinah and accepted Islam.

Questions:

1. What was the relative strength of the Muslim army and

the enemy in the Battle of Hunayn?

2. Describe the role of the holy Prophet ﷺ when the Muslim army fell under intense pressure?
3. How did Shaybah ibn 'Uthman become a Muslim?
4. What led to the siege of Ta'if, and how did it end?

CHAPTER 34

EXPEDITION OF TABUK

It came to the knowledge of the leader of both worlds, the holy Prophet Muhammad ﷺ, that the Byzantine Empire (eastern half of the Roman Empire) was busy accumulating a substantial fighting force in Syria and were making considerable preparations to launch an attack on the city of Madinah. Hence, the holy Prophet ﷺ gave the order to prepare for battle. Rather than waiting here and before the Byzantine forces come to Madinah, the Muslims should go to them and confront them there. The wealthy Muslims were asked to donate and contribute to the war effort generously, so that necessary arrangements could be made for provisions and riding animals for the Muslim army.

GENEROSITY OF ABU BAKR AL-SIDDIQ

Abu Bakr al-Siddiq put all the wealth and possessions that he had together in a bundle. A large amount of items were put together in his bundle as well as four thousand *dirhams* (silver coins). He came with his possessions to the holy Prophet Muhammad ﷺ and placed everything at his feet.

Seeing this self-sacrifice and generosity of his friend, the holy Prophet ﷺ asked: "Have you left anything for your family?" Abu Bakr replied: "I have left Allah and His Messenger at home for them." The late poet-philosopher of Islam, Allama Muhammad Iqbal (d. 1938), records this scene beautifully:

Sufficient for the moth is the lamp, for the nightingale the rose;
For al-Siddiq however, sufficient is Allah and His Messenger!

Generosity of 'Umar al-Faruq

'Umar ibn al-Khattab al-Faruq divided all his wealth and possession into two equal halves. He took one half and brought it to the holy Prophet Muhammad ﷺ. The embodiment of mercy, the holy Prophet ﷺ, asked: "O 'Umar! Have you left anything for your family?" He replied: "O Allah's Messenger! I have brought half of my wealth for you and left the other half at home for my family."

On that day, 'Umar al-Faruq realised that he was unable to supersede Abu Bakr al-Siddiq in any endeavour, since he had brought all his wealth and 'Umar had brought half.

Generosity of 'Uthman al-Ghani

'Uthman ibn 'Affan al-Ghani catered for ten thousand Muslim soldiers by providing animals to ride, weapons, armours and other necessities of battle. Ten thousand *dinars* (gold coins) he donated and handed over to the pride of both worlds, the holy

Prophet Muhammad ﷺ. The holy Prophet ﷺ was moving his hand through the *dinars* and supplicating: "O Allah! Be pleased with 'Uthman. I am pleased with him. It matters not to 'Uthman whether he performs any deed from today."

GENEROSITY OF ABU 'AQIL AL-ANSARI

When Abu 'Aqil al-Ansari heard the leader of both worlds, the holy Prophet Muhammad ﷺ, encouraging people to donate and financially contribute, he looked around his home and found absolutely nothing that he could present to the holy Prophet ﷺ. He went to see a Jewish man who owned an orchard. Abu 'Aqil made an agreement with him that he would work to irrigate his orchard by continuously taking bucket after bucket of water from the well. In return for this labour, the owner of the orchard would give him two *sa'* of dates (a *sa'* is an ancient measure of weight). Abu 'Aqil spent the whole night repeatedly taking buckets of water out of the well and emptying them, and by the time it was morning, he had irrigated the whole orchard. The owner gave him two *sa'* of dates. Abu 'Aqil left one *sa'* of dates for his family at home and took one *sa'* of dates and presented them as a donation in front of the holy Prophet ﷺ.

The noble master, the holy Prophet Muhammad ﷺ, did not dishearten Abu 'Aqil for bringing only one *sa'* of dates. What need of the Muslim army could this small contribution actually fulfil? Rather, he honoured and encouraged him. The holy Prophet ﷺ then instructed a Companion to take these dates that Abu 'Aqil had presented, and where the donations had been gathered and were being prepared for the Muslim soldiers, he was to put two dates on each pile of provisions.

The holy Prophet ﷺ said that due to the blessing of Abu 'Aqil's sincerity, Almighty Allah will accept the donations of all others too.

In short, all of the Muslims made contributions according to their individual circumstances. Women also took off their jewellery, gold bracelets, necklaces, ankle bracelets, and their rings, and presented them to the holy Prophet ﷺ in order to cover the costs of the Muslim army.

JOURNEY TO TABUK

The leader of both worlds, the holy Prophet Muhammad ﷺ, departed from Madinah heading for Tabuk in the month of Rajab in the ninth year after the emigration (*hijrah*). The weather at that time was very hot with the sun blazing during the day. The whole country was also experiencing severe drought and famine. But, in spite of that, these thirty thousand Muslim soldiers embarked on a journey of seven hundred kilometres heading for the plain of Tabuk for only one purpose; to raise the glory of Islam.

On arrival in Tabuk, the holy Prophet ﷺ sent an envoy to the Byzantine Emperor, Heraclius, inviting him again to Islam. In response, Heraclius sent a message saying that he was a follower of the holy Prophet ﷺ, but he could not give up his throne and crown. Hearing this, the holy Prophet ﷺ said: "The unfortunate Heraclius has spoken a lie."

During his stay in Tabuk, the holy Prophet ﷺ sent delegations and envoys to numerous tribes in that region. Consequently, many tribes entered into peace treaties with the holy Prophet

ﷺ and agreed to the leadership of the Muslims by paying the *jizyah* (state levy) in return for security, guaranteed peace and protection of person and property. The army of Islam remained in Tabuk for twenty days. When the Byzantine Emperor could not find the courage to confront the Muslims, the holy Prophet ﷺ announced his departure from Tabuk and returned to Madinah.

Mosque of Dirar

Around the time of the expedition of Tabuk, the hypocrites in Madinah had built a mosque near the Quba Mosque in an effort to organise their activities, use as an operational base and deceive the Muslims. On his return from Tabuk, the holy Prophet Muhammad ﷺ was met on the outskirts of Madinah by the hypocrites who said: "The mosque we had built is so that the people who are ill or disabled as well as those who cannot go to *Masjid Nabawi* (Prophet's Mosque) during the rainy season and the dark summer nights, they will be able to perform their prayers in congregation here. We very much wish that you, the holy Prophet ﷺ, come to this mosque, lead us in prayer and supplicate for blessings for us." All these statements and assertions were based on sheer deceit and hypocrisy. The ulterior motive was that the presence of the holy Prophet ﷺ in their mosque would legitimise its existence and result in a large number of simple-minded Muslims flocking to it. In this way, the hypocrites thought they would be able to trap naïve Muslims in their deceit quite easily.

Allah Almighty prohibited His beloved Messenger, the holy Prophet Muhammad ﷺ, from going to this mosque because its foundations were laid upon mischief and unbelief, and it was not built on piety. It became clear that the building in the guise of a mosque, referred to as the Mosque of Dissension (*Masjid Dirar*), was a centre of conspiracy and sedition against the Muslims. The holy Prophet ﷺ then ordered for this building to be demolished and burnt down to the ground. He further instructed that rubbish, dead animals and rotten objects be thrown in its place.

Pilgrimage of the 9th Year AH

In the ninth year after the emigration (*hijrah*), three hundred Muslims set off from Madinah to perform the pilgrimage (*hajj*) in Makkah. The holy Prophet Muhammad ﷺ appointed Abu Bakr al-Siddiq as their leader. During the days of the pilgrimage, Abu Bakr would deliver a sermon every day at various stations of the pilgrimage and would inform the pilgrims about matters concerning the rituals and religious duties to be performed at these stations. 'Ali ibn Abi Talib reports that when the holy Prophet ﷺ sent him to perform the pilgrimage in the company of Abu Bakr, the holy Prophet Muhammad ﷺ had instructed him to make the following four announcements:

1. No individual other than the believer (*mu'min*) will enter Paradise. Unbelievers will not be able to attain eternal salvation.
2. No man or woman will be able to circumambulate around the Ka'bah in a naked state.
3. Those who have entered into treaties with the holy Prophet ﷺ will be able to exercise their rights for the duration of the treaty until it expires.
4. After this year, polytheists (*mushrikun*), i.e. those who

associate partners with God, will not be able to perform the pilgrimage and approach *Masjid Haram* (Sacred Mosque) in Makkah.

Death of the holy Prophet's Son, Ibrahim

In the month of Rabi' al-Awwal in the tenth year after the emigration (*hijrah*), the holy Prophet Muhammad's son, Ibrahim, passed away. He was one year and four months old at the time. At his death, tears began to flow from the blessed eyes of the holy Prophet ﷺ and he said: "These tears are a sign of mercy. The one who does not show mercy to others does not receive any mercy either. I prohibit people from wailing and from recounting such virtues which are not found in the deceased. Our hearts are saddened. But, in spite of this, we do not let any word slip out of our tongue that might lead to the displeasure of our Lord."

The mercy for the world, the holy Prophet ﷺ, instructed for Ibrahim to be buried in the cemetery of *al-Baqi'* in Madinah. The holy Prophet ﷺ himself led the funeral prayer, which was performed with four *takbirs*. After he had been buried, the holy Prophet ﷺ sprinkled water over the grave. This was the first grave that had water sprinkled over it.

The day Ibrahim died, there was a solar eclipse. People circulated widely the rumour that it was as a result of grief and sorrow that the sun had eclipsed. When the holy Prophet ﷺ heard of this, he said: "The sun and the moon are two great signs of the divine power of Almighty Allah. Their eclipse is not caused by anyone's death."

Questions:

1. Describe the generous donations of Abu Bakr al-Siddiq and 'Umar al-Faruq during the preparations for the expedition of Tabuk.
2. What was the donation of Abu 'Aqil, and how was he able to acquire what he donated?
3. What was the background to *Masjid Dirar*?
4. Who led the pilgrimage which took place during the ninth year after emigration?
5. What did the holy Prophet ﷺ say at the death of his son, Ibrahim?

CHAPTER 35

FAREWELL PILGRIMAGE

In his lifetime, the holy Prophet Muhammad ﷺ performed one pilgrimage (*hajj*) and four lesser pilgrimages (*'umrah*). In the tenth year after the emigration (*hijrah*), when the holy Prophet ﷺ decided to perform the pilgrimage, an announcement was made in settlements and villages where Muslims were residing that this year it would be the mercy for the world, the holy Prophet ﷺ, himself who will be leading the caravan. Consequently, a large number of caravans began arriving in Madinah to be part of this pilgrimage, to the extent that the grounds around Madinah became filled with tents of the guests of Almighty Allah who will be travelling on the pilgrimage to Makkah.

On the day of Saturday 25th of the month of Dhu'l-Qa'dah, after the noon (*zuhr*) prayer, this caravan departed from *Masjid Nabawi*. At the *miqat* of Dhu'l-Hulayfah (which is the station a few miles outside of Madinah from where the state of pilgrim sanctity begins), the holy Prophet ﷺ entered into the state of pilgrim sanctity wearing the *ihram* (pilgrim dress) intending for both *hajj* and *'umrah,* and began reciting the *talbiyah* (pilgrim recital). The multitude of people in all four directions as far as the eye could see began to repeat the prayer. With their echo, the mountains, trees and deserts all began to resonate. Eventually, after travelling for eight days, this blessed caravan entered *Masjid Haram* (Sacred Mosque) on Sunday 4th of Dhu'l-Hijjah. After performing *'umrah,* the holy Prophet ﷺ stayed in Makkah for a few days and on the 8th of Dhu'l-Hijjah, he went to Mina to perform the *hajj* rituals.

During this pilgrimage, the holy Prophet ﷺ had quite clearly let it be known that this was his last meeting with the people at this specific place. After this occasion, they will not be blessed with such an opportunity. Since the holy Prophet ﷺ bid farewell to his community (*ummah*) in this pilgrimage, for this reason it is called the Farewell Pilgrimage (*hijjat al-wada'*). On this occasion, the final verse of the Qur'an was revealed in which Almighty Allah announced the completion of religion:

ٱلْيَوْمَ أَكْمَلْتُ لَكُمْ دِينَكُمْ وَأَتْمَمْتُ عَلَيْكُمْ نِعْمَتِي
وَرَضِيتُ لَكُمُ ٱلْإِسْلَـٰمَ دِينًا ۚ

"On this day, I have perfected for you your religion, and have completed My favour upon you, and have approved Islam as the religion for you." [*Qur'an* 5:3]

The holy Prophet ﷺ brought one hundred camels with him for the sacrifice. Of these, sixty-three camels were slaughtered by the holy Prophet ﷺ with his own blessed hands. The holy Prophet's age at that time was also sixty-three years old, and so he sacrificed one camel for each year. The remaining thirty-seven camels were slaughtered by 'Ali on the instruction of the holy Prophet ﷺ. The holy Prophet ﷺ then instructed that the meat and the hides be distributed amongst the poor.

At the completion of the sacrifices in Mina, the holy Prophet ﷺ called for a barber to shave off the hair on his blessed head. All believers gathered around the holy Prophet ﷺ in the hope of collecting some of his hairs for blessing. The barber distributed the blessed hairs amongst the people. Some people were able to gain one hair, others gained two strands of hair. Khalid ibn al-Walid got hold of some hair from the holy Prophet's blessed forehead, which he securely placed inside his hat. During the Battle of Yarmuk, one day his hat went missing. He ordered everyone to search for the hat saying: "In this hat is the blessed hair of the holy Prophet ﷺ. Whenever I have taken part in any battle wearing this hat, Allah has always granted me victory."

The following is a summary of some of the points mentioned in the various sermons that the holy Prophet Muhammad ﷺ delivered at different stations during this pilgrimage:

"All praise is for Almighty Allah. O people! Indeed your Lord (Allah) is one and your father (Adam) is one. There is no superiority of an Arab over a non-Arab, nor of a non-Arab over an Arab, nor of a white over a black, nor a black over a white, except by God-fearingness (taqwa). In the court of Almighty Allah, the most honourable of you is the one who is the most God-fearing."

"Almighty Allah has made your lives, your property and your honour, as sacred as this day of yours, in this month of yours, in this city of yours. All Muslims are brethren; brothers to one another."

"I enjoin upon you the good treatment of women, for they are a trust from Almighty Allah with you. You have rights over them and they have rights over you."

"I am leaving you with two things, which if you hold unto them firmly, you will never go astray: the Book of Almighty Allah (Qur'an) and the practice of His Prophet (sunnah). "

"Those who are present here, let them convey my message to those who are absent. Perhaps the one to whom this message is taken understands and remembers it better." The holy Prophet ﷺ then asked: "Have I conveyed the message?" The Companions responded: "O Allah's Messenger! Indeed you have." The holy Prophet ﷺ then said: "O my Lord! Be witness that I have conveyed Your message to Your Creation."

Questions:

1. What is the number of pilgrimages and lesser pilgrimages the holy Prophet ﷺ performed in his life?
2. What did Khalid ibn al-Walid do with the holy Prophet's blessed hairs?
3. Mention some of the points from the holy Prophet's Farewell Sermon?

Chapter 36

Last Days

Following his return from the Farewell Pilgrimage, the holy Prophet Muhammad ﷺ spent the months of Muharram and Safar (of the year 11 AH) in the city of Madinah. During this time, one day he went to visit the graves of the martyrs of Uhud. There he prayed for their forgiveness. Then the holy Prophet ﷺ returned to *Masjid Nabawi* (Prophet's Mosque) and delivered his final sermon sitting down on the pulpit. The following are a few sentences from that sermon:

"I am to lead and go before you, and I will bear witness over you. You and I will meet at the fountain of kawthar, and sitting here I am looking at the fountain of kawthar. I have been given the keys to the treasures of the earth. I have no fear that after me you will commit shirk (polytheism) by associating a partner with Allah. But I am certainly afraid that you will try to surpass each other in acquiring worldly riches."

A point to consider here is that those people who accuse the

Ahl al-Sunnah wa'l-Jama'ah of committing *shirk*, how will they interpret these clear words of the holy Prophet ﷺ?

Illness Commences

During the last days of the month of Safar, the holy Prophet Muhammad ﷺ experienced headaches. Severe headaches were followed by fever. The fever was so intense that heat could be felt by touching the top of his head band. The intensity of the fever would cause unconsciousness. Seven water bags carrying water from different wells were poured over the blessed body of the holy Prophet ﷺ, which reduced the intense fever and the holy Prophet ﷺ felt slightly better. In spite of this illness and physical weakness, the holy Prophet ﷺ continued to lead the daily prayers himself up to four days before his death. When the holy Prophet ﷺ could no longer go to the mosque as a result of the illness and pain increasing, he sent a message saying:

مُرُوا أَبَا بَكْرٍ فَلْيُصَلِّ بِالنَّاسِ

"Instruct Abu Bakr to lead the people in prayer."

In this way, the holy Prophet Muhammad ﷺ, during the days of his illness, appointed Abu Bakr al-Siddiq as his deputy (*khalifah*) in leading the daily prayers and himself performed prayer behind him too.

A Day Before Death

Sayyidah 'A'ishah al-Siddiqah, the mother of the believers,

states that during the illness, the holy Prophet Muhammad ﷺ asked her: "O 'A'ishah! Where are those *dinars* (gold coins)?" She quickly got up, brought the eight *dinars* that they had and presented them to the holy Prophet ﷺ. The holy Prophet ﷺ moved the *dinars* around in his hand for a while and then said: "O 'A'ishah! If I meet my Lord having left these *dinars* in my house, then what will my Lord say that My servant did not have trust in Me? 'A'ishah! Immediately distribute these amongst the poor." Consequently, she took even the last trivial bit of wealth that was in the house of the Beloved of Almighty Allah and distributed it amongst the poor and needy.

This was the state of the home of that blessed soul, the holy Prophet Muhammad ﷺ, who had been granted the keys to the treasures of the earth, such that even during the final night of his life, there was no oil to light a lamp with. Sayyidah 'A'ishah reports that she sent her lantern to one of her neighbours asking her to place a few drops of oil in their lantern so that they could at least get through that night.

This worldly poverty of the holy Prophet Muhammad ﷺ was something chosen by him. The holy Prophet ﷺ by his own volition and desire gave no importance to such worldly possessions and riches, and he devoted his entire life for the pleasure of his generous Lord.

Once the archangel Jibril (Gabriel) entered into the presence of the holy Prophet ﷺ and said: "Almighty Allah sends greetings of peace to you and asks that if you would like Him to turn these mountains into gold, and wherever you go, they move with you?" The holy Prophet Muhammad ﷺ replied: "O Jibril! This world is home for a person who has no other home, and this wealth is for him who has no wealth. Only that person seeks to gather this world together who is deprived of intellect and wisdom."

One day, the mother of the believers, Sayyidah 'A'ishah, brought out a ragged Yemeni piece of cloth, used for wearing round the waist, and a blanket with patches of cloth sewn together. Taking an oath, Sayyidah 'A'ishah said: "It is in these two cloths that the holy Prophet ﷺ departed from this world towards his Lord."

FINAL MOMENTS

The archangel Jibril came to the holy Prophet Muhammad ﷺ and said: "Almighty Allah sends greetings of peace to you. The angel of death is standing at the door seeking permission to come inside." The holy Prophet ﷺ replied: "The angel of death is granted permission to enter."

When the angel of death entered the room, he stood in utmost respect and said: "O Allah's Messenger! Almighty Allah has sent me to you and ordered me that I obey every command of yours. If the holy Prophet ﷺ permits me to take his soul, I will do so, but if you do not grant me this permission, I shall leave with the pure soul left intact in the blessed body."

The holy Prophet ﷺ granted the angel of death permission to take his soul. Sayyidah 'A'ishah al-Siddiqah narrates that she was holding the holy Prophet's blessed hand and was caressing his blessed body with it. Suddenly, the holy Prophet Muhammad ﷺ withdrew his hand from hers and said with his blessed tongue:

رَبِّ اغْفِرْ لِي وَأَلْحِقْنِي بِالرَّفِيقِ الْأَعْلٰى

"O my Lord! Forgive me, and unite me with the Supreme Companion."

Sayyidah 'A'ishah states: "At the precise moment when the holy Prophet's blessed soul left his pure body heading towards the Supreme Companion, I sensed a special kind of fragrance which I have never experienced to date."

The holy Prophet ﷺ passed away at the age of sixty-three years on the day of Monday, the 12th of Rabi' al-Awwal, at the time between mid-morning and the beginning of the time for noon (*zuhr*) prayer. He passed away on Monday and was buried on the following Wednesday night.

On the 12th of Rabi' al-Awwal, Abu Bakr al-Siddiq led the dawn (*fajr*) prayer in *Masjid Nabawi*. The holy Prophet Muhammad ﷺ had been feeling better that morning, so Abu Bakr went home. The death occurred close to midday. On receiving this devastating and upsetting news, Abu Bakr immediately headed for the holy Prophet's Mosque. There, he found the noble Companions in an intense state of grief. In particular, 'Umar ibn al-Khattab was in shock and not in control of himself.

Abu Bakr went straight to the holy Prophet's room. He lifted the sheet off the holy Prophet's blessed face, kissed the radiant forehead, fell into tears and said: "You are dearer to me than my mother and father. If it was in our control, we would lay down our lives for you. If you had not ordered us to refrain from wailing over the deceased, I would have cried so much that fountains of tears would have flowed from my eyes." Then he supplicated: "O Allah! Convey our salutations and greetings of peace to your Beloved. O Allah's Messenger! Remember us servants in the court of your Lord."

The hypocrites began to say that if the holy Prophet ﷺ had been a genuine Prophet, he would not have died. Already in a state of sheer grief at the separation from his noble Beloved and then this insulting remark from the enemies, 'Umar ibn al-Khattab lost control of himself in sadness and sorrow. He unsheathed his sword and started to say: "If anyone says that Allah's Messenger has died, I will split him into two with this sword." Abu Bakr al-Siddiq quickly moved forward and encouraged 'Umar to adopt the path of patience and then he recited the following verse from the Qur'an:

وَمَا مُحَمَّدٌ إِلَّا رَسُولٌ قَدْ خَلَتْ مِن قَبْلِهِ ٱلرُّسُلُ ۚ

"And Muhammad is only a Messenger. Surely there have passed away many Messengers before him." [*Qur'an* 3:144]

HIS CHILDREN AND WIVES

The holy Prophet Muhammad ﷺ had three sons and four daughters. The three sons are Qasim, 'Abdullah and Ibrahim; and the four daughters are Zaynab, Ruqayyah, Umm Kulthum and Fatimah al-Zahra'.

Ibrahim was born from the blessed womb of Sayyidah Mariyah al-Qibtiyyah and all the other children were born from Sayyidah Khadijah. All three sons died in their childhood, but the four daughters lived and witnessed the era of prophethood and embraced Islam.

It was after the death of Sayyidah Khadijah that the mercy for the world, the holy Prophet Muhammad ﷺ, married on numerous occasions to establish cordial relations with various other tribes, in order to extend the scope of the propagation of Islam and to make it more effective. All of these pious wives are the mothers of all believers, and it is due to these fortunate and blessed women that the knowledge of countless matters relating to Islam reached the Islamic community (*ummah*).

The following are the names of the pious wives of the holy Prophet Muhammad ﷺ:

1. Sayyidah Khadijah bint Khuwaylid
2. Sayyidah Sawdah bint Zam'ah
3. Sayyidah 'A'ishah al-Siddiqa bint Abi Bakr
4. Sayyidah Hafsah bint 'Umar
5. Sayyidah Zaynab bint Khuzaymah
6. Sayyidah Umm Salamah Hind bint Abi Umayyah
7. Sayyidah Zaynab bint Jahsh
8. Sayyidah Juwayriyyah bint al-Harith
9. Sayyidah Umm Habiba Ramlah bint Abi Sufyan
10. Sayyidah Safiyyah bint Huyayy
11. Sayyidah Maymunah bint al-Harith

The holy Prophet ﷺ also had another wife named Sayyidah Mariyah bint Sham'un al-Qibtiyyah, who was initially a bondmaid, and she is the one who gave birth to the holy Prophet's son, Ibrahim.

Burial Preparations

The blessed body of the holy Prophet Muhammad ﷺ was washed without removing his clothes. His shroud consisted of three white sheets. The room in which he passed away, there a grave was prepared. A red coloured blanket was spread out in the grave, on which the holy Prophet ﷺ was laid to rest.

Fadl ibn 'Abbas stated: "When the holy Prophet ﷺ was placed in his radiant grave, that is when I saw his blessed face for the last time. I noticed that his blessed lips were moving, so I placed my ears close to his blessed mouth. I could hear that the holy Prophet ﷺ was saying:

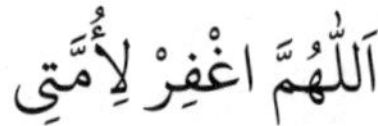

"O Allah! Forgive my community." "

Fadl continues: "When I informed the other Companions of this, they were amazed at the affection and mercy the holy Prophet ﷺ had for his followers."

Funeral Prayer

The leader of both worlds, the holy Prophet Muhammad ﷺ, stated: "After washing and enshrouding me, place me next to my grave, and then for some time everyone should vacate the room. First of all, the angels will perform my funeral prayer." Consequently upon his passing away, in accordance with the holy Prophet's instruction, his body was enshrouded and then placed in his room as all the people vacated the room.

Afterwards, the men and women from the holy Prophet's pure household (*ahl al-bayt*) entered the room and presented prayers and salutations of peace and blessings. After them, Abu Bakr al-Siddiq and 'Umar al-Faruq accompanied by a few people from the *ansar* (helpers) and the *muhajirun* (emigrants) entered the room and presented their prayers and salutations of devotion with the following words:

اَلسَّلَامُ عَلَيْكَ أَيُّهَا النَّبِيُّ وَرَحْمَةُ اللهِ وَبَرَكَاتُهُ

"Greetings of peace be upon you, O Prophet! And the mercy of Allah and His blessings."

When this group of people came out, another group entered and this process continued until all the men had completed their funeral prayer in this manner. Afterwards, women and after them children were allowed inside. In this way, all people, group after group, gained this privilege. Nobody was leading this funeral prayer.

To recite prayers and salutations of peace and blessings upon the holy Prophet Muhammad ﷺ is such a great action that it always keeps the relationship of an individual with the holy Prophet ﷺ fresh and continuous. A notable Companion of the holy Prophet ﷺ, namely Abu Darda', narrates that the holy Prophet ﷺ said: "Send abundant prayers and salutations of peace and blessings upon me on Fridays, for on this day the angels come into my presence and present to me the prayers and salutations of the one who recited them." Abu Darda' asked: "O Allah's Messenger! As long as you are alive and present in this world, until then certainly the angel present them to you, but how will they present them to you after you have died?" The mercy for the world, the holy Prophet ﷺ replied: "Almighty Allah has made it forbidden on the earth to consume the pure bodies of the noble Prophets. A Prophet of Allah remains alive and he is given sustenance."

In another narration, the holy Prophet ﷺ said: "There is none who recites prayers and salutations upon me except that I hear his voice wherever he may be."

Questions:

1. During the final days of the holy Prophet ﷺ, why did Abu Bakr al-Siddiq begin leading the Companions in prayer?
2. Describe the state of the holy Prophet's house in terms of its wealth before he passed away, and what happened to the small amount of *dinars* that were in the house?
3. List the names of the holy Prophet's children and his pious wives.
4. Describe how the funeral prayer of the holy Prophet ﷺ was performed, and where was he buried?

CHAPTER 37

DEVOTION TO THE FINAL PROPHET ﷺ

BELIEF OF IMAM MALIK

Once the Muslim ruler, Caliph Mansur Abu Ja'far, came to *Masjid Nabawi* (Prophet's Mosque) and began having a conversation with Imam Malik. Soon Imam Malik said: "O leader of the Muslims! Do not raise your voice in this mosque, for Almighty Allah has warned the people not to raise the voice above that of the holy Prophet Muhammad ﷺ, lest they lose all their good deeds without even realising the loss."

It is clear from this that the respect and manners towards the holy Prophet ﷺ required during his lifetime, the same respect and manners are to be observed after his death too.

After hearing this from Imam Malik, the Caliph Mansur immediately lowered his head, and then he enquired whether he should face in the direction of the *qiblah* (prayer direction towards the Ka'bah in Makkah) when making a supplication or should face the holy Prophet Muhammad ﷺ? Imam Malik replied: "Why do you turn your face away from the holy Prophet ﷺ when supplicating, whereas the holy Prophet ﷺ is an intermediary (*wasilah*) for you as he was for your father, Prophet Adam [*as*]? You should supplicate and make *du'a* facing the holy Prophet ﷺ and ask him for his intercession (*shafa'ah*), for Almighty Allah says:

وَلَوْ أَنَّهُمْ إِذ ظَّلَمُوٓا۟ أَنفُسَهُمْ جَآءُوكَ فَٱسْتَغْفَرُوا۟ ٱللَّهَ وَٱسْتَغْفَرَ لَهُمُ ٱلرَّسُولُ
لَوَجَدُوا۟ ٱللَّهَ تَوَّابًا رَّحِيمًا ﴿٦٤﴾

"And if these people when they have wronged their souls come to you (O my beloved), and seek forgiveness from Allah, and the Messenger seeks forgiveness for them, they will surely find Allah the most Relenting, ever Merciful." " [*Qur'an* 4:64]

FINALITY OF PROPHETHOOD

The holy Prophet Muhammad ﷺ is the last and final Prophet of Almighty Allah in the sacred system of prophethood (*nubuwwah*). With him the sequence of prophethood has come to an end, and he is the Prophet until the end of time. The holy Prophet ﷺ himself announced this fact when he said: "The chain of prophethood has ended, and no other Prophet or Messenger will come after me."

LOVE FOR THE HOLY PROPHET ﷺ

Love for the holy Prophet Muhammad ﷺ is the soul of Islam and the essence of faith (*iman*). The mercy to the world, the holy Prophet ﷺ, said:

لَا يُؤْمِنُ أَحَدُكُمْ حَتَّى أَكُونَ أَحَبَّ إِلَيْهِ مِنْ وَالِدِهِ وَوَلَدِهِ وَالنَّاسِ أَجْمَعِينَ

"None of you can truly become a believer until I am more beloved to him than his parents, his children and all other people."
[*Sahih al-Bukhari*]

Love for His Family

The following are some traditions from the holy Prophet Muhammad ﷺ concerning his pure family (*al*) and pure household (*ahl al-bayt*):

1. The holy Prophet ﷺ once held the hands of his grandsons, Hasan and Husayn, and said: "Whoever loves me, loves these two children and loves their father and mother, will be with me on the Day of Judgement and in my station."

2. The holy Prophet Muhammad ﷺ said: "I am leaving you with two such things that if you hold on to them firmly, you will not go astray: the Book of Almighty Allah and my household."

3. By the blessing of recognising the rights of the pure family of the holy Prophet ﷺ, a person gains salvation from the fire of Hell. Having love for the pure family of the holy Prophet ﷺ becomes a means of crossing the bridge of *sirat* with ease on the Day of Judgement. Assisting and cooperating with the pure family of the holy Prophet ﷺ leads to protection from divine torment and punishment.

LOVE FOR HIS COMPANIONS

The mercy for both worlds, the holy Prophet Muhammad ﷺ said: "Any person who even hurls verbal abuse towards my Companions, he is cursed by Almighty Allah, His angels and all humanity. Almighty Allah does not accept his repentance nor anything given by him in compensation (*fidyah*)."

A man once said to Mu'afi ibn 'Imran that the status of the later Muslim ruler, 'Umar ibn 'Abd al-Aziz, was greater than that of the Companion, Amir Mu'awiyyah. He immediately responded: "Nobody can ever be compared to the noble Companions of the holy Prophet ﷺ. Amir Mu'awiyyah was a Companion of the holy Prophet ﷺ, he was a scribe of the divine revelation and he was a custodian of the revelation of Almighty Allah."

A funeral was once brought before the holy Prophet Muhammad ﷺ so that he could lead the funeral prayer. The holy Prophet ﷺ did not perform the funeral prayer of that person and said: "The deceased had dislike towards 'Uthman al-Ghani, and so Almighty Allah has made him disliked."

SUPERIORITY OF THE LEARNED

The mercy for both worlds, the holy Prophet Muhammad ﷺ said: "Almighty Allah is the most Generous, and I am the most generous amongst the descendants of Prophet Adam [*as*], and after me the most generous is that person who acquired knowledge and then spread that knowledge. On the Day of Judgement, when Almighty Allah will raise that learned person from his grave, he will not be standing as a mere individual, rather he will stand in the status of the entire community (*ummah*)."

INTERCESSION

On the Day of Judgement, when all human beings will be gathered together in the resurrection ground, at that time the sun will be very close above their heads. People will be suffering in a state of sorrow and unbearable agony. After a long wait, they will consult with one another and decide to go to some great personality who will on this day be able to offer intercession (*shafa'ah*) on their behalf in the majestic court of Almighty Allah.

Eventually, all people will go to Prophet Adam [*as*], then to Prophet Nuh (Noah [*as*]), then to Prophet Ibrahim (Abraham [*as*]), then to Prophet 'Isa (Jesus [*as*]), and they will tell them about the terrible state they are in and ask them to intercede on their behalf in the court of Almighty Allah. However, all of the noble Prophets will refuse to do so. In the end, they will tell the people to go to the generous presence of the Prophet of the last time, the holy Prophet Muhammad ﷺ. Consequently, the people will come to the holy Prophet ﷺ and ask him to intercede for them. To which, the beloved Prophet ﷺ will say:

أَنَا لَهَا . أَنَا لَهَا

"I am for the intercession, I am for the intercession."

Thereafter, the holy Prophet Muhammad ﷺ will fall into prostration before the majesty of Almighty Allah. A voice from

Almighty Allah will call out: "O my beloved! Raise you blessed head from prostration and ask me. Whatever you ask me, I will grant you. Whoever you will intercede for, I will accept your intercession in his favour."

Abu Hurayrah narrates that every Prophet was granted one particular supplication (*du'a*), the acceptance of which was guaranteed by the Lord of all the worlds, Almighty Allah. All of the noble Prophets have utilised this particular supplication in this world, but the holy Prophet Muhammad ﷺ said: "I have saved this accepted supplication so that on the Day of Judgement I can utilise this supplication by asking for intercession in favour of my *ummah*."

اَلْحَمْدُ لِلّٰهِ رَبِّ الْعَالَمِينَ

وَالصَّلَاةُ وَالسَّلَامُ عَلٰى سَيِّدِ الْمُرْسَلِينَ وَعَلٰى آلِهِ وَأَصْحَابِهِ أَجْمَعِينَ

O Lord of all the worlds! O the utmost Kind, the ever Merciful!
Grant Your mercy and the intercession of your Beloved ﷺ to me, my parents, my children, my relatives, my teachers, my students, my friends, my well-wishers, and all the benefactors of Jamia Al-Karam.

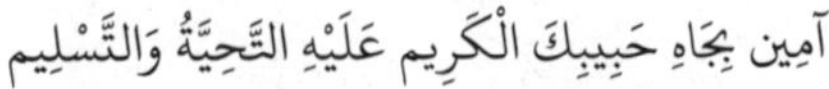
آمِين بِجَاهِ حَبِيبِكَ الْكَرِيم عَلَيْهِ التَّحِيَّةُ وَالتَّسْلِيم

Muhammad Imdad Hussain Pirzada
Friday, March 12th, 1999
Jamia Al-Karam, Retford, United Kingdom

www.alkarampublications.com

www.alkarampublications.com